"Superusers are actually this generatic

Scott Crawford, Principal, LMN Architects

"In this book, Randy has identified a class of people who are the harbingers of a new era of building."

Ian Keough, father of Dynamo, CEO of Hypar,
from the book's Foreword

Superusers

Design technology is changing both architectural practice and the role of the architect and related design professionals. With new technologies and work processes appearing every week, how can practitioners be expected to stay on top and thrive? In a word, Superusers.

Superusers: Design Technology Specialists and the Future of Practice will help you identify who they are, the value they provide, and how you can attract and retain them, and become one; what career opportunities they have, what obstacles they face, and how to lead them. Written by Randy Deutsch, a well-known expert in the field, this is the first-ever guide to help current and future design professionals to succeed in the accelerating new world of work and technology.

Providing proven, practical advice, the book features:

* Unique, actionable insights from design technology leaders in practice worldwide
* The impacts of emerging technology trends such as generative design, automation, AI, and machine learning on practice
* Profiles of those who provide 20% of the effort but achieve 80% of the results, and how they do it
* What will help firms get from where they are today to where they need to be, to survive and thrive in the new world of design and construction.

Revealing the dramatic impact of technology on current and future practice, *Superusers* shows what it means to be an architect in the 21st century. Essential reading for students and professionals, the book helps you plan for and navigate a fast-moving, uncertain future with confidence.

Randy Deutsch AIA, LEED AP is the Associate Director for Graduate Studies and Clinical Associate Professor at the University of Illinois Urbana-Champaign, USA, teaching and conducting research in design, professional practice, building technology, and digital technology. Randy is an international keynote speaker, workshop leader, and design technology authority. An architect responsible for the design of over 100 large, complex sustainable projects, Randy has been an Exec Ed program leader at Harvard GSD. He has written for *DesignIntelligence*, has been featured in *ARCHITECT* magazine and *Architectural Record*, and is the author of three books: *Convergence: The Redesign of Design* (2017) on the nature of the ongoing convergence of technology and work processes in the profession and industry; *Data Driven Design and Construction: Strategies for Capturing, Analyzing and Applying Building Data* (2015, translated into Chinese in 2019) on the innovative individuals and firms who are leveraging data to advance their practices; and *BIM and Integrated Design: Strategies for Architectural Practice* (2011, translated into Chinese in 2018) tracking the social and organizational impacts of the new technologies and collaborative work processes, among other publications. More at www.randy deutsch.com.

Superusers

Design Technology Specialists
and the Future of Practice

RANDY DEUTSCH

Routledge
Taylor & Francis Group

LONDON AND NEW YORK

First published 2019
by Routledge
2 Park Square, Milton Park, Abingdon, Oxon OX14 4RN

and by Routledge
52 Vanderbilt Avenue, New York, NY 10017

Routledge is an imprint of the Taylor & Francis Group, an informa business

British Library Cataloguing-in-Publication Data
A catalogue record for this book is available from the British Library

Library of Congress Cataloging-in-Publication Data
Names: Deutsch, Randy, author.
Title: Superusers : design technology specialists and the future of practice / Randy Deutsch.
Description: New York : Routledge, 2019. | Includes bibliographical references and index.
Identifiers: LCCN 2018042735| ISBN 9780815352594 (hb : alk. paper) | ISBN 9780815352600 (pb : alk. paper) | ISBN 9781351138987 (ebook)
Subjects: LCSH: Architectural practice. | Design–Practice. | Architecture–Technological innovations. | Technology–Social aspects.
Classification: LCC NA1995 .D59 2019 | DDC 720.28–dc23
LC record available at https://lccn.loc.gov/2018042735

ISBN: 978-0-815-35259-4 (hbk)
ISBN: 978-0-815-35260-0 (pbk)
ISBN: 978-1-351-13898-7 (ebk)

Typeset in UniversLTStd
by Swales & Willis Ltd, Exeter, Devon, UK

Cover Photo Credit: TIM GRIFFITH for LMN Architects

To all those who share this path, an offering from a fellow traveler

Contents

Acknowledgments

This book could never have been realized without the distinctive voices of the Superusers themselves featured herein. I wholeheartedly thank Ian Keough for his forward-thinking Foreword; Shane Burger, Matthew Krissel, Stephen Van Dyck, Scott Crawford, Jordan Billingsley, Ana Garcia Puyol, Cory Brugger, Ryan Cameron, Hilda Espinal, Brian Ringley, Dan Anthony, Hiram Rodriguez, Fernando Araujo – *Superusers all* – for their selfless contributions and sharing of insights, and for serving themselves – through their words and actions – as exemplars of the design technology leadership described in these pages. This book wouldn't exist without them. For my Routledge (and Taylor & Francis) publishing team: a hearty thanks to Fran Ford, Publisher, Architecture, and to Jennifer Schmidt, Senior Editor, Architecture who immediately recognized the promise in the book's premise and championed the proposal to fruition; to Trudy Varcianna, Senior Editorial Assistant, Architecture for her always attentive assistance and responsiveness throughout; to David Moore, Editorial Assistant Built Environment, Architecture. Lastly, for his assistance in coming up with and completing the diagrams that grace this book, Matthew Ross, appropriately enough – at the time of this writing – an architectural studies major with a computer science minor. He has big goals for his future.

Foreword

At this moment, we are at the confluence of a healthy economy and the growing existential crisis of the architectural profession considering its relationship to automation. The pattern that has taken hold during the last several economic cycles has become increasingly clear. When the economy is healthy, venture capital is unlocked for startups to solve specific problems in industry, and architecture firms begin to invest in research and development, loosening the requirement that all explorations be specifically project driven. The result of this loosening is the creation of an environment in which Superusers who seek to automate our industry create the tools and processes which push us forward.

Many who read this book will be scared by the description of the Superuser. Superusers understand the reality that much of what we do in architectural practice can and should be automated, but they work in a profession which has its roots in an artistic tradition spanning hundreds of years. This tradition assumes, I would argue erroneously, that the act of "design" is irreducibly human. What Superusers have identified is that, in an environment of ever-shrinking fees, the only path to our salvation is through automation. And any discussion of automation implies the reduction of the human workforce. The Superuser will be seen by some as a direct challenge to their livelihood. This natural response, which is historically shortsighted, would come as a surprise to a Superuser. Because Superusers don't often self-identify. From their perspective, they're just having fun solving challenges and saving people time.

The Superuser is therefore a heroic character as she fights the often backwards and inept processes by which buildings are designed and constructed, doing so from within, but also a melancholy character in that she works in an environment which is often unable to fully perceive her value or compensate her commensurate with her contribution both to the firm and to the profession. She hears stories every day of how the world around her is being transformed by technologies like machine learning, and sees start-ups leveraging millions of dollars in venture capital to automate everything from the parsing of building codes to the construction of modular housing. With each passing economic cycle the amplitude of investment in startups in our industry increases, causing our Superuser to consider, "should I seek greener pastures?"

This book comes at a critical moment. It enumerates the characteristics of the Superuser, so that we can identify these individuals in our own environment before they seek those greener pastures. It postulates how we might reward and accelerate the developments of the Superusers so that they understand how critically important what they are doing is for our practice. And it begins to imagine an environment in which Superusers run the show. What will our profession look like when the best among us, those who are asking fundamental questions about the place of technology in architecture, are the leaders?

In this book, Randy has identified a class of people who are the harbingers of a new era of building. In reading Randy's description of how these Superusers are often underutilized, and in suggesting ways that we can more fully incorporate these individuals into current practice, I'd argue Randy hasn't gone far enough. Perhaps the flow of Superusers out of the profession to startups which more fully appreciate their skills, is the natural process of renewal by which our profession will be broken down and built up again.

Perhaps instead of identifying ways that we can retain Superusers, given the means that we have traditionally applied for retaining employees – more money, more status, etc. – we should be identifying ways that we can accelerate their exodus. In their current roles they will always be swimming against the tide. It is, paradoxically, in the nature of Superusers to never be satisfied, so attempts to placate Superusers with the means the industry currently has, will only forestall the inevitable exodus of these users to startups which don't suffer from the existential crisis in trying to define their industries, and exist purely to provide tools which create a step change of technological progress.

If we don't accept this vision of our industry being disrupted from outside, then we need to use this guide to identify the Superuser, and we need to let them lead us. Speaking from some experience, I can say that the future they are envisioning is very different from the one our industry has currently set for itself. For this reason, the path will be rocky. But there's no such thing as a gentle disruption.

by Ian Keough, Father of Dynamo, CEO of HYPAR

Preface: scaring the pants off of everybody

Thanks for presenting last week and scaring the pants off of everybody.

Scott Lelieur, Director of Operations at Lake|Flato Architects, had participated in the Design Colloquium at the Presidio Officers' Club in Presidio Park in San Francisco, CA, where I spoke in 2018. First established in 1776, for 200+ years the Presidio served as an army post for three nations, world and local events, from military campaigns to World Fairs and earthquakes, and California has long set the national agenda on culture and technology.[1] It was about to, relatively speaking, experience its latest cataclysm: a talk on AI and its impact on the future of the design professions and building industry.

It really shouldn't have come as a surprise, as the Colloquium theme, after all, was *Disruption: Game-Changing Design.* Attended by leaders of "Design-First" firms in architecture, engineering, and related design disciplines, the attendees were decidedly not all *technology-first* professionals. The Colloquium coined the term *Design-First* to refer to "practices that have maintained a consistently high level of design quality, while not dependent on a black-cape superstar."[2] The list of firms that have attended and participated in the Colloquium since the late 2000s reads like a veritable who's-who of celebrated architectural and engineering design firms not led by a *starchitect*: Behnisch Architects, Bohlin Cywinski Jackson, Ennead Architects, FXCollaborative, Herbert Lewis Kruse Blunck, Olson Kundig Architects, Miller Hull Partnership, Pugh + Scarpa, Studios Architecture, Snøhetta, William McDonough + Partners, ZGF Architects, and Lake|Flato Architects, among others.

On the first day, the session immediately following lunch was entitled, *Exploring the Future for Architects, Engineers and Designers*. The session's speakers and panelists included Craig Curtis, *President of Katerra*, and Luis Jaggy, *Design Researcher, Woods Bagot Super-Space, and myself*. As the first speaker, I spoke about the growing technology haves-have nots situation among firms; about AI and automation in architecture; about the unavoidable changes we're about to experience as a profession and industry, and made recommendations for how we can arrive there empowered, unscathed, and still playing at the top of our game.

Speaking in Northern California where wildfires have been increasingly prevalent, I showed a slide of a recent wildfire and asked the crowd:

See that fire on the horizon? That's AI. And it's fast approaching. Too fast to fight or respond to, it's coming for your office. Why wait for a fire we cannot put out, when there are things we can be doing today to prepare us for the inevitable conflagration of AI?

It was this that earned me Scott Lelieur's *thanks for presenting . . . and scaring the pants off of everybody*.

It was never really my intention to scare the pants or any other clothing article off anybody – but to provoke, incite conversation, and ideally action.

My other main purpose was to introduce those present to the concept of Superusers: the folks who'll help us get to where we need to go.

Superusers to the rescue

Design professionals are experiencing a shift right now, and some are more comfortable with it than others. In order to increase productivity, profits, and frankly our chances of survival, we *all* need to get comfortable with it. We are about to see incredible changes in our profession and industry, and Superusers – as you're about to read – are the ones who will get us there: mostly unscathed, and for the lucky few, triumphant. Who they are, how they do this, what value they provide, and how you can attract and retain them, is the subject of this book.

Firms have witnessed the transition to, and integration of, design technology since the late 1980s, and will continue to do so for the foreseeable future. This is not new. But how this transition will be impacted by the cutthroat economic scenarios of the near future, including increased competition, rising automation, lowering wages despite increasing productivity, commoditized services, and thinning margins, represents clear and present threats – and opportunities.

After CAD and BIM, the developed design world is entering the third generation of digital technology. Still very much a work-in-progress (*take a breath*), the age of automation, built on advances in virtual reality, artificial intelligence, robotics, and going by various names – the age of technology; the information age; the computer age; the age of computation; the 4th industrial revolution; the second machine age; the robotic age – relies on the architect's gold, data, and also tools: software, algorithms, and soon, working alongside robots and architect-machine collaboration. We are entering a world where the architects' relationship to computers and other machines, and to software and other digital tools, is leading to one of two outcomes: in the near future, the design professional will be an Augmented and Informed (AI) architect – call it, as Douglas Engelbart has, the *augmented architect* – collaborating with machines. Or, they'll be competing with AI and robots: call it *toast*.

We may not know how this will play out through the 2020s, but we do know who will shepherd the rest of us to a successful resolution: *Superusers*.

This book will help you to identify *Superusers*; what differentiates them, what their superpowers are, what roles they play within organizations, and the value they provide; where to find them, how to hire them, or grow them internally, engage and retain them; what career opportunities they have, and what obstacles they'll face, and how to lead them, and answer what technology has to do with designing exceptional buildings.

Despite the *users* in Superusers, this book is *not* a technology book: it is not about design technology. It is about the people who are able to achieve magic with the technology we have – by working with, through, and among others – and create the tools we need, in order to achieve the results firms are striving for – no matter what their goals or ambitions may be. LMN Architects partner, Stephen

Van Dyck, himself a widely recognized industry authority in the adoption of emerging technologies, sums up the aim of design technologists and the focus of the book pointedly when he says of Superusers, "It's all, ultimately, about filling performance goals from both an aesthetic and a functional perspective, but also from a financial perspective. And I would argue that the widespread proliferation of this approach across the industry is fueled by necessity." He assures us, "It is impossible in this day and age to be a successful firm operating at scale without technology being part of the equation." As I made clear in my Colloquium talk, this goes for Design-First firms as well.

How will we get there?

What will help us get from where we are today to where we need to be, to survive and thrive in the new world of design and construction, is the subject of this book. What will help us get there are *Superusers*, the individuals that provide 20% of the effort and achieve 80% of the results; who take an assignment that normally takes a week and complete it in just hours.

Superusers provide a great deal of value to teams and firms – financial, performative, liability-reducing, architectural design excellence, value. They're firefighters and fixers, whose work is – as many mention – *noble*. They're the ones who connect the dots; get obstinate, uncooperative, and non-communicative tools and platforms to talk to each other; often winning jobs for the firm with their tech wizardry, demonstrating to owners how computation will make their buildings better.

Whether rationalizing column placement or facades, or calculating body carbon; whether maximizing views, or fresh air, or proximity, Superusers are design professionals with the wherewithal to recognize a tool, curiosity to inquire into a tool, confidence to mess with a tool, capacity to learn a tool, creativity to combine tools, and the interpersonal intelligence to connect with others to achieve actionable results.

These are the individuals who are misunderstood, undervalued, hard to find, and once found, hard to keep – and keep happy – hard to promote, and hard to fit into the organization, with its traditional titles, roles, and paths to promotion. This book addresses how successful firms today are addressing these concerns to remarkable results.

One of the key values offered by this book is the easy to apply Superuser concepts – the ten C-factors; ten Superuser superpowers; Superusers as this generation's generalist architect; as force multipliers; as the "Other," and as 5-tool players; *storytelling through technology*; the design technology specialist career path as risk journey; benefitting from working in the grey space; *eyes-on/hands-off; eyes-on/hands-on*; and *minds-on/everything else is off* hybrid roles; the Architect Development League (ADL); the *third space*, among many others – dispersed throughout the book you're about to read.

The premise of this book is simple: design technology specialists are not the "Other," and design technology will not – if you just wait it out – become permanently obsolete. It's like the carnival game of whack-a-mole: try as one might to absorb technology into firm workflows and work processes, a new one pops up *ad finitum*. Design technology – and design technologists, the individuals who leverage, master and create these technologies – aren't going away any time soon and remain an integral part of projects, teams, and firm success. If you're lucky.

This book will show you how, more often, to be lucky.

Why this book?

Why write, if this too easy activity of pushing a pen across paper is not given a certain bull-fighting risk and we do not approach dangerous, agile, and two-horned topics?[3]

I wrote this book because, since the late 2000s, I have been immersed in the world of design technology, consulting, recruiting, meeting, speaking, and sparring with, observing, and hearing from firm leaders – and leaders-in-the-making – about their concerns related to technology in the workplace, and over time have built an ever-widening network of committed, engaged, and enterprising design technologists. In that time, I have researched practice and recognize, as you do, that something must change. I also recognize that what we *don't* need is another book on the technology itself (or for that matter on computationally generated pavilions!) but instead one on the individuals who are getting results for their organizations and helping an industry to get from point A to point B (and B-yond).

As an author, architect, professor, and head of a graduate school in a major architecture program with global ties; as someone who led a tech-forward Harvard GSD Exec Ed program, and as an international keynote speaker, my experience remains: firms want both power-user (billable) skills as well as blue sky strategy (overhead) skills – in *the same person*. This almost impossible to come by person and personality, a veritable unicorn, is the *Superuser*, and this book will tell you how to find them, if necessary, how to *make* them – and if you are one – how to make the most of your career prospects, *without having to leave the profession or industry*.

Like my three previous books – all published in the same disruptive decade – this fourth utilizes practice-based research, featuring worldwide doers and leaders working in design technology. And yet, this book is something of a departure in that it doesn't so much address the process and the tools as the people who make them and make them possible. In this book I allow the multifarious voices of the Superusers come through, providing interpretation and analysis as needed.

I came to write the book because I believe, along with others, that the architecture profession and design industry will look radically different by 2030; and design technology specialists – a particular high-performing, high-functioning, highly connected, and highly motivated vocal minority here called Superusers – represent the near future of our industry. They're the Sherpa who will get us to where it is we're trying – as teams, firms, profession, and industry – to go.

And while no one can say exactly what that place will look like, I believe that the one thing that will get us there are design technologists and design technology leadership: *you*. That is the subject of this book: the caring and feeding of Superusers so they can help us to get to where we need to go, *and fast*. This urgency – to address an intractable, seemingly unsolvable, non-obvious problem all firms are facing – is why there is a need for this book now. Since the late 2000s we have seen the use of technology migrate into all aspects not only of life but also of the building lifecycle, from design and documentation to fabrication and construction, to communication and facilities management, operations, and maintenance. Buildings are increasingly complex and expensive, and design teams are under greater pressure to improve costs, timelines, and efficiency while remaining innovative, achieving higher quality, and importantly, *meaning* in their work. For the first time, owners can have it all, so they want it all. Superusers deliver on their demands.

Since the latest downturn of the economy, employees have been expected to do the work of two or three. Fees are down, processes need to be more efficient, with each employee required to be increasingly more productive. But how?

How, in other words, will we get from here to there – where we need to be – and pronto?

In a word, *Superusers*.

Notes

1 www.nytimes.com/2018/06/02/opinion/sunday/california-progressive-politics.html.
2 http://designcolloquium.com.
3 José Ortega y Gasset, *On Love: Aspects of a Single Theme*, Eastford, CT: Martino Fine Books, 1957.

Introduction

How a specialist came to be this generation's generalist architect

Architecture and engineering (AE) firms are experiencing a crisis, brought about by failures of communicating their ultimate value, putting forward a competitive value proposition and viable business model, and an inability to assert their relevance. The people who could arguably lead these firms into the future – addressing and resolving these and other crises – are leaving the industry for startups and so-called vertically integrated companies (verticals) such as WeWork and Katerra, Autodesk, Disney and Amazon, among others. The problem, they say, is that AE firms can't pay them enough to stay.

But economic and existential considerations are only part of the cause. More important than adequate remuneration, these firms haven't been able to promise these future leaders a future. Today's leaders haven't paved a path for design technology specialists to firm leadership that takes their gifts and ultimate value to the organization – let alone the industry – into consideration.

Irrespective of their role, finding and nurturing talent remains the most critical concern for architecture, engineering, and construction organizations, while attracting, retaining, and developing our firms' future leaders present both intractable challenges and unlimited opportunities. Besides going the traditional CTO or CIO routes, there is little precedence for design technologists to rise to and attain leadership positions within design firms. Thus, they are leaving our field for greener – i.e. more remunerative – pastures.

It is time we stanch the flow out of our industry – and this book proposes how.

Figure 0.1 Every Friday afternoon KieranTimberlake holds Knowledge Community meetings to share new workflows and discoveries made by project teams. Here, researchers demonstrate projection mapping. (2018) Credit: KieranTimberlake.

Superusers defined

First, who are these design technology specialists and leaders, and what distinguishes them? They are our Superusers, design professionals who leverage tools and technology to do more, and be more, *with the people skills* to accomplish all they do with and by means of others, often to astonishing results.

Unlike the CAD, BIM, and IT-related roles that preceded them, their focus is on skillsets *and* mindsets; on hard skills *and* soft skills; on the specialist's depth *and* wide social wingspan; on technology *and* design; on computation *and* multifarious interdisciplinary skills, leading our teams, firm, and industry into the future. At the risk of oversimplifying, they're specialists with interpersonal intelligence, an ability to understand emotional behavior in others and leverage it to achieve results.

You may be one of them, or seen them: at Autodesk University, BILT, SmartGeometry, Acadia, or other industry events. They're graduates of Stevens Institute, ETH, design technology programs such as that at Harvard GSD, and other institutions of higher learning. You've listened to them on the designalyze podcast, or donated with them to Colin McCrone's gofundme after his 2018 bike crash. They're seemingly everywhere – and nowhere. They're Superusers, and they're what we will all need to aim to become to be a design professional in the 2020s and beyond.

A Superuser isn't just another name for design technology specialist or computational designer. Superusers differ from proficient software users, or for that matter, from high-performing design professionals. Because being a "specialist" only tells half the story. That's because, "Superusers," says Scott Crawford, Principal at LMN Architects, "are actually this generation's version of the generalist architect."

An imperfect perfect appellation

Superusers. It's an admittedly imperfect perfect label. For starters, the word "user" can have a negative connotation – conjuring the image of a drug user, where technology is their drug of choice. "There's always been a stigma attached to the word *user*," argues Hilda Espinal, Chief Technology Officer at CannonDesign. "When I think of the term Superusers I think maybe I'm not even a 'user' at all," says Dan Anthony, Design Computation Leader, NBBJ. "Sometimes when I think about my designers, I think about them as my users. And that would make me not a user."

Despite the term's inclusion of *user*, Superusers are not people sitting at a computer seeming to singlehandedly put a building together by hitting macros with their left hand while holding a sandwich in their right (though these folks certainly exist, and this book features one). Instead, with an emphasis on *Super*, a Superuser is somebody who, in addition to the requisite skillsets, is gifted with emotional intelligence and, when challenged with a problem, has the wherewithal to figure out what expert to go to; who serves as a liaison between IT and somebody with a problem that needs addressing; somebody who's curious and who can connect the dots. As Dan Anthony explains:

> That's a strong hypothesis to explore, because it pokes around the edges of this distinction, both in defining something that people may not like, but also in defining something that may be an opportunity or opening in this whole practice.

The title "design technologist" may be too limiting because it contains the word design. Titles seldom pinpoint what we do as design professionals, especially now as technology continues to evolve. Take Dan Anthony's title. Is being a Design Computation Leader similar to being an enlightened BIM manager? Anthony explains:

> Yes, right now we treat computational method as a compliment to BIM. In some ways, it's an artificial distinction, and becoming more and more so every day. But at the same time, we have a BIM manager on a project. They end up being a little more tactical due to their role. BIM managers are often also more useful day to day, since computation isn't always in play in a project.

Is Superuser an unnecessary label and/or distinction? An identity is important to distinguish the folks from those who primarily address IT, technology, and tools, at the expense of human qualities. For if anything, as we'll soon see, Superusers are all about their distinguishing human qualities, and while they diminish pain points and connect uncooperative tools, improving processes and workflows, they exist first and foremost in service not to the technology but to fellow design professionals: *people.*

Given how quickly design practice is evolving, does "design technologist" still accurately describe this person or role? Is the title necessary? "Yes, it's necessary," says Brian Ringley, Senior Researcher at WeWork, continuing:

> It's necessary both practically, the way the industry has turned out so far, and historically, but I also think it's just necessary in theory. What I mean by that is, there's always been a specialist, at least as long as I've been in practice, whether that's a CAD manager or somebody who specialized in BIM. There's always been something thought to be extra-technological to the architectural delivery process, certainly all the more so today, from design computation and programming, custom applications for practice and delivery, to still having traditional BIM manager roles.

All Superusers share certain traits – but each Superuser also represents a special case. Again, take Dan Anthony. Does he see himself and self-identify as a design professional, design technologist, or part of IT? He explains:

My role is both defined and amorphous. The official title on paper is that I am a Design Computation Leader at the firm level. Which puts me under our Chief Information Officer, CIO Paul Audsley. Myself and two other people – currently Marc Syp and Nate Holland are Design Computation Leaders – we sit in different studios. Our goal is to organize all of the different efforts in every studio across the firm. There are currently about 12 people in our group that do this kind of work, with the three of us leading the way.

The book explores how to identify and where to find Superusers; and when you can't find them, how to make them, and better yet, how to become a Superuser yourself. We'll look at habits of high-functioning Superusers, how firm leaders leverage Superusers as in-house consultants or integrate Superusers on teams, keep Superusers energized and engaged, and from leaving for startups.

In terms of the hiring and promotion of Superusers, discussed in more detail in a later chapter, most firms have placed traditional architecture jobs squarely into three boxes: project designer, project architect, and project manager. But what if your career path doesn't fit cleanly into any of these three boxes? What implication does that have for promotion? Jordan Billingsley of Hord Coplan Macht is a design technology specialist. He might also answer to computational designer, or even computational BIM manager. So, where do these titles fall in our typical three boxes? According to Billingsley:

Designer can't really make it to computational BIM manager, but a designer could make it to a computational designer, where they're doing more parametric modeling. A project architect would be a good computational BIM person, because they understand what information's important, and they just lack those skills of how to lift that out of a project. I'm not sure that there's a computational side to being a project manager. The project manager, if it would splinter off into a design technology role, would be a design technology director, where they're not experts on how to use any of the tools, but they can see the direction of the industry, and they know how to fight within their firm to get time protected for training and for onboarding.

Following this logic enables Billingsley to splinter off three boxes into six, opening a way for discussion of future promotion.

Superusers is about design technologists and who they need to become to lead teams and firms. Superusers leverage technology – but they do so as much for their distinctive skillsets as for their mindsets, attitudes, and emotional intelligence. In fact, of the ten defining features that make up a Superuser (as explained in Chapter 1), no fewer than nine are considered soft skills. In the past, they may have gone the project designer, project architect, or even project manager route. But in many cases these fields were crowded – especially around the time of the last economic downturn – so they turned to technology as an opportunity to stand out from the crowd, to deliver value, but also as a career differentiator. This choice – in some cases, a deal with the devil – has implications for their identity, fulfillment at work, as well as their career paths and opportunities for promotion. The amount of risk this requires on their part is discussed at length in a later chapter – and, importantly, labeled with a memorable moniker.

The book in three parts

In Part one, Chapter 1 looks at the Superusers' C-Factors, the qualities and attributes that make these superpowers possible. The

Figure 0.2
Exploded
Skin study
for UC
Riverside
Recreation
Center.
(2018) Credit:
CannonDe-
sign.

attributes – ten X-factors starting with the letter C and described in this chapter – are the bedrock for what separates Superusers from someone who specializes in technology. We look at what drives Superusers and their defining qualities. In the research for this book, ten distinguishing features or attributes common to all Superusers were mentioned, and observed, again and again. Superusers exhibit a predilection and expertise, not only at the technologies they master but, perhaps more importantly, the aforementioned finesse at human interaction. While design technologists and computational designers are needed for their output, it is in the end their outlook and consideration for other's interests and needs that truly separate them from ordinary technologists.

Chapter 2 looks at ten Superuser superpowers to look for when identifying people for your team. These superpowers cover problem-solving and communication skills, including interpersonal and conversational skills, question-asking, thought leadership, and storytelling. Next, we look at the most often-mentioned superpower, teachability, or a thirst for learning; not applying computational processes but how to think computationally, identify repeatable tasks, and how to recognize when to ask, "Is this something we can automate?" We'll also look at entrepreneurialism and how Superusers contribute to something bigger. Finally, the chapter ends with intangibles – hard-to-define qualities that all design technology specialists share, their employers recognize, value, and reward – and looks at Superusers as *5-tool players* in architecture.

There are certain "tells" in design professionals that cause them to stand out. "I grew up in a rural area and you can figure out who's a farm kid and who's a city kid," says Ryan Cameron, Project Architect at DLR Group. "Not everybody knows everything. I'm willing to admit that about myself. Everybody's got their niche." The mindset of the design technologist is *I'm going to integrate these new technologies into standard practice to elevate practitioners so that the definition of practice is dynamic.*

Chapter 3 focuses on the roles Superusers play on teams and in firms, each in an effort to determine which are more prevalent and which more effective, resulting in more value for firms. The chapter opens by looking at Superuser roles as they compare with more traditional titles and roles within AE organizations. Next, we compare and contrast the differences between generalist vs.

specialist design technologists, the generalist/specialist hybrid role, and how teams and firms benefit from this grey space. The chapter next looks at whether Superusers provide the most value when billable (where e.g. computational design should be billed on a project) vs. overhead; when integrated on teams vs. sitting in the corner; and, hands-on vs. primarily strategic, providing leadership in a management role. The chapter concludes looking at the role of the Superuser in practice in a Superuser team case study. We've covered the ten Superuser qualities and ten Superuser super-powers. Now it's time to put these skills into action. This chapter looks at the roles Superusers play on teams, in firms, and in the industry. Firm after firm, Superusers roles fall into predictable categories: either generalists or specialists, or sometimes along a continuum. Design technology specialists often serve as internal consultants, where they are considered overhead, or integrated into project teams, and billable, or some combination.

Superusers – and their employers – see what they do in terms of providing value. Part two opens with Chapter 4, looking at the value Superusers bring to their teams and deliver in terms of increased productivity, via agile processes, automation, and automating repetitive processes. Next, we look at the impact of AI and at two potential professional paths where we'll either be augmented and informed (AI) vs. being fully automated (AI). We'll also discuss how Superusers provide an improved user experience, by easing use and accessibility of tools, while connecting tools, people, and processes, reducing user pain points. The chapter concludes looking at how Superusers seek out and leverage new technologies and participate in software developments, tool creation, and the potential commercialization of these tools.

Chapter 5 looks at the hiring (and poaching) of Superusers, the seemingly never-ending search for design technologists – finding, recruiting (and the reality of looting or pilfering) – Superusers. Next, we'll look at leadership and design technologist buy-in and hiring Superusers as a design challenge. The chapter concludes with hiring for tool virtuosity vs. soft skills. Today, design technologists – and especially design technology leaders – are expected to be both hands-on and to have a strategic outlook from which the firm can benefit. Filling this role, while never easy, has become easier. Some of my own architecture major students who minor in computer science would be ideal candidates for such a role. Following the advice and suggestions in this chapter should make the process easier still. Some firms, especially those who have seen how hard it can be to hire from outside their firm, opt to grow them from within. The key thing is to keep constantly on the lookout, not just when you're in need of filling a position, and not to let finding a promising candidate with lesser technology skills dissuade you from having a conversation. They may just turn out to be the very person your firm so badly needs.

Engaging and retaining Superusers really has to do with the proper care and feeding of Superusers: how do you keep them, and keep them from leaving for richer pastures?

Chapter 6 opens with the ways firms keep things moving, interesting, and relevant for design technologists. Next, we look at when Superusers leave architecture, engineering, and construction (AEC) firms for startups and other industries, why they leave startups for AEC, and how firms compete with these startups for Superusers. The chapter concludes with a look at training and upskilling of Superusers. Technology specialists in AEC are a special breed, and engagement is about retaining these valued employees. The usual go-to tactics – an attaboy/attagirl, or gift card – just won't cut it. Engaging and retaining Superusers involves nurturing the 10 Cs, the soft skills, mindsets, attitudes, and hard skills possessed by every Superuser.

The career paths of Superusers vary. Part three opens with Chapter 7 covering the career paths and Superuser risk journey, the qualifications for career advancement of design technology specialists, including leveraging your talent for tech on building design projects, leveraging your architect status for a role in tech, and leveraging your talent for tech on managing people. Next, we look at the career *risk journey* of design technologists. For computational designers, by not following the traditional path, they take on a lot of risks career-wise, and the professional trajectory becomes more of a risk journey rather than a career path. Finally, we'll look extensively at the career provenance of Superusers – including emerging, mid-career, and firm leaders; including the IT path, BM manager path, and internal consultant role – through career path case studies. At the same time, they have commonalities. Challenges of some

Superusers include how to keep one's hands on the technology while minimizing the managing of people. Others accept the role of people, budget, and schedule management as an inevitable part of becoming a firm leader. No matter the specifics, Superusers are the next generation of the profession.

Having looked at design technologists as architects and managers, Chapter 8 focuses on design technologists who are, or aspire to become, designers: digitally savvy designers who are computationally savvy, influencing the design process through computational means. Design technologists who also design, or who become full-time designers, leveraging their talent for technology on building design projects. Design technologists who have an interest in being a designer, whether technology is an impediment or expediter to their becoming designers. Do designers, technical project architects, or managers represent the future of design technologists? The chapter concludes with a look at *the third space*, where design technologists are proactively designing the design process. Design and technology. A false dichotomy at the start by the artificially siloed college curricula and largely perpetuated by the profession. Additionally, technology has been misused in the formal obsession with weird and twisty buildings and complex geometry, and a too-narrow and sterile definition of optimization. Design technologists return technology to design, figuring out how to incorporate both analog and digital technology into projects, team workflows, and their firms' work processes – not for its own sake but to improve the design, functionality, and affordability of projects. They're always looking for opportunities for technology to make them better designers. Earlier defined, more rapidly iterated, higher-quality design.

Part three concludes with Chapter 9 which looks at the leading of Superusers: what design technology leaders do, what it takes to lead and support Superusers, and the need to identify what is advancing in our space that we're not seeing, staying relevant, and the regular need for skill rebuild. It looks at what it takes to create an environment that fosters a computational mindset from one's team. The chapter closes with marketing a firm's use of technology, and winning projects by emphasizing technology and the Superusers who create and use it. When design technology specialists become design technology leaders, there's an understandable shift in priorities and responsibilities. This chapter explains in what way and how.

As with all of my books, *Superusers* is based on practice-based research. Unless otherwise indicated, all quotes are from the author's own interviews with these individuals that took place in 2018. *Superusers: Design Technology Specialists and the Future of Practice* makes the case that design technology specialists are this generation's generalist architects – reason alone that firm leaders need to take them seriously and give them their uninterrupted attention. This book aims to help start this critically important conversation.

Part one

Why Superusers?

Chapter 1

Superusers' C-factors

In the research for this book, certain distinguishing features or attributes common to all Superusers were observed, again and again. Superusers exhibit a predilection and expertise, not only for the technologies they master but finesse with human interaction. While design technologists are needed for their computational skills and productivity, it's their outlook and consideration for others' interests and needs that separate them from ordinary specialists.

This chapter looks at the qualities and attributes that make the Superusers' superpowers of Chapter 2 possible. These attributes – ten X-factors starting with the letter C – are the bedrock for what separates a Superuser from someone who specializes in technology. The chapter looks at what drives Superusers, their defining qualities, and sought-after differentiators.

Curiosity

Superusers are naturally curious – they're driven by curiosity – particularly about the world outside of technology. It is not enough for technologists to focus exclusively on mastering technology and tools – for that to be the end of their interests. Some address this by adding "A" for *art* to STEM subjects, making it STEAM. "I'd add a 'd' for design and make it STEAMD," says Dan Anthony, Design Computation Leader, NBBJ. "We need design. I'm personally very enthusiastic about the [Stanford] d.school approach. Experientially solving problems. Hacking out a process. Sometimes the exposure to the arts can be very narrow or cursory if you don't want to apply it." Anthony explains how curiosity led him to study architecture in the first place:

One of the things that came out of my experience at Stanford is an interest in graphic design – something I've always been interested in. One of the things that got me to the University of Oregon is that I continued to explore that space after I graduated from Stanford. I found that the thing that I wanted to learn more about was architecture and design. I went to California College of the Arts (CCA) for classes. I travel and go to museums, draw and photograph buildings. I realized I was gravitating toward the urban space and wanted to learn how to design it. I was driven by curiosity.

Superusers' interests outside of technology have a positive impact on their work, providing perspective, enhancing their laser focus on a task, making their work more enriching by leveraging alternative reference points. And, as will be discussed in a later chapter, curiosity remains a valued characteristic that employers look for in design technologist candidates. "You're just looking for curiosity," says Brian Ringley, Senior Researcher at WeWork where he leads research efforts in the areas of construction automation and robotics, playing a pivotal role in developing and testing new methods of building manufacturing and working collaboratively with WeWork's design, construction, and logistics teams. He continues:

You're not looking for somebody who needs to be told what to do. You're looking for somebody who has an extremely large appetite for knowledge. It's not even problem solving so much. It's just gaining knowledge, and the way you gain knowledge is to locate problems and wonder why it's a problem, and decide if it's a problem worth solving or if the problem is the problem. You're just hungry for knowledge, you have that appetite and you're a naturally curious person; if you have that attitude, that you should be able to pick things up. That's how I felt about myself and that's what I've noticed over the years, the students who are the highest performers are those who don't wait for me to demo a tool. They have a problem that they want to solve and they go about solving it.

Outside of WeWork, Ringley recognizes the difficulty in nurturing curiosity in his students in the courses he teaches on data-driven parametric design, interoperable workflow convergence and vertical integration, and robotic automation for architectural manufacturing at Pratt Institute's Graduate Architecture and Urban Design (GAUD) program:

> I teach a lot of Grasshopper as part of various courses and it's a good proxy for design computation and smart models and process in general, as well as also just being a useful skill to know Grasshopper. I know I should be more practical about it, but I'm just always heartbroken that people aren't trying to figure things out and asking questions. It just seems like they, by and large, come in and it's like they did what they needed to do to get to that point.
>
> I've had a lot of advantages in my life so I don't want to hold myself up, like everybody should be the same type of person I've been. I remember one advantage being that I learned Rhino in high school, which is a freak accident mostly. I remember just being bored with the assignment and being like, "I'm going to type in every command. I'm going to run every Rhino command and I'm just going to see what it does." I tell my students that and they're like, "Oh, Grasshopper's so hard," whereas I said, "Just put a random component down and see what it does, and then put another one, and just do that once a day, and just see what that leads to." As an educator, that's always been that really, really difficult thing to attain, which is "How do I nurture curiosity?" rather than "How do I deliver content?"

Curiosity can also help develop one's ability to adapt to change – something of particular import given how quickly technology and processes change today. "That goes with the curiosity, because inevitably that's going to lead you to try new things," explains Ringley, citing his leaving Woods Bagot for WeWork:

> It's like coming to WeWork. It was hard not to notice them, and it was hard not to notice they were doing the types of things I wanted to do and they were really, really good at it. That's exciting and that curiosity takes over and you're like, "Well, I have to go do that now because that seems like where all the smart people went, and where all the big things are happening within this industry, so I'll pop in over there and see what happens."

Contextualizers

Woods Bagot Principal Shane Burger has talked in the past about object intelligence, situational intelligence, and systemic intelligence in terms of building components. Could these three qualities be a way of describing the people you want to work with? "In a way, it's talking about the different scales of collaboration, communication, or connection," says Burger. "There's always that moment when someone has to put their head down, their headphones on, block out the world, and get something done. But at the same time, I never want somebody who cannot contextualize their work."

Contextualizers look at their work in larger contexts that spiral out from the problem they are trying to solve, beyond themselves to larger and larger reference points. Contextualizing means to always ask what does my work mean beyond what I am working on now, in ever-increasing questions of *beyond*? Burger adds:

They ideally know what this means for their individual project. Hopefully they do, beyond themselves. What does this mean for the work I'm doing now? What does this mean for the larger project team? Beyond that, what does this mean for this typology or this sector? Is there something here I can learn from? Beyond that, what does this mean for the practice, or even beyond that?

Connectors

Arguably, people enter the AEC industry because they like working with things, objects, or places, not for the interaction with people. For some, *people* are an unavoidable liability of working in a profession or industry.

There are a surprising percentage of Superusers that could be considered people-persons. They like people, are energized – not drained or exhausted – by being around people, and thrive in an environment where they daily have the opportunity to be in service to others. Skilled in pattern recognition, their interest in serving others goes a long way to help explain why Superusers are – whether connecting people, tools, processes, or just the dots – considered *connectors*. Shane Burger explains:

That is a big part of what I do. I constantly look for connections and problems to solve. Sometimes applying something that

Figure 1.1
**Wynyard
Walk. (2018)
Credit:
Woods
Bagot.**
Image credit ©
Trevor Mein

happens over in the Perth office to something that happens in London. I absolutely encourage the team to do that. I don't want them to become overwhelmed. You don't want to over-weight the individual task that they are doing at that time that then might be used to solve 10,000 other problems. That's where there are two mindsets between the 50/50 of the work. The one 50% that's focusing on the individual project, and the other 50% that's to say, *alright, let's back up. Let's look at this from a 10,000 foot view. What am I doing now that can go bigger?*

Here's an example of what is meant by connection. "We were seeing a lot of problems happen on projects related to some aspects of interoperability and some very common workflows from Grasshopper into Dynamo into Revit that were happening on a very regular basis," explains Burger. He continues:

Because we were using Flux at that time, we added on top of that some concerns about where Flux was going from a big picture point of view. That then turned into Brian Ringley and Andrew Heumann building some aspects of the Wombat toolkit that we then released publicly. These were some utilities that we were using again and again and again in the practice. We didn't see anyone else with them out there. They are not really that complicated in terms of IP, but they are really handy utilities. Where this went after this was saying OK, now wait a minute. We've fixed some of that for us. But is that really a long-term solution? Additionally, we have this design research group based in our Sydney studio called SuperSpace that is running into similar paradigms, but not quite the same solution space. There are some similar conversations happening. That then sparked a conversation around, let's start thinking about a future system that might be similar to Flux. We started having very serious conversations with the team from Speckle, in particular Dimitrie Stefanescu. We started talking with Jonatan Schumacher with where Konstru was going in its next steps. That went from single project tools, to multi-project tools, to enterprise tools that we pulled out, developed, and then released, to then start thinking about platforms. So it went at that point from plug-ins to platforms. That's a good conversation to have. I don't want to saddle a particular project with a platform-level conversation, but there does need to be that moment where you can back-up and think at platform and infrastructure level, asking: how does this actually impact how we do our work on a regular basis? And is there some amazing opportunity that we could have by thinking about it at platform level?

Communicators

How do colleagues and firm leaders inside the office become aware of Superusers' superpowers? "They probably walked past my desk and said, 'Hey, what's that?' And I said, 'here, watch this.' That was how it happened," says Ryan Cameron, Project Architect at DLR Group who actively shares what he is working on, online and off, with others. He says:

We have an Intranet that all the big firms have. I will post occasionally, "For the next episode of Dynamo Next we have this going on. Here are some cool things we can do with data, some basic steps you can learn."

When it comes to communicating what design technologists or computational designers do, many clients wouldn't know what to ask for. So it falls on Superusers to be able to clearly explain what it is they do, what problems they can solve, and just what value they bring to assignments, projects, and their clients. It may be hard to communicate the focus of one's work to outsiders when design technology is focused on internal research and development. Early schematic design on a project would fall within the firm's visualization guru, or architectural designer, explains Jordan Billingsley, BIM Coordinator with Hord Coplan Macht:

> We would only need to bring in the computational designer when they've settled on rough rules for what the design of the façade should be, and then trying to get a transparency versus opacity percentage, and that's when you'd need the computational designer, which would still be in the CD phase, so at that point you've already got the client to agree to do something more computational.

Superusers are able to get the word out to others, whether via intranets and internal presentations, or by hosting parties at industry events, teaching in a university, delivering a podcast, participating in public speaking, engaging in social media, or being featured in articles and books. WeWork's Brian Ringley does, or has done, all of these. He says:

> Your personality is your personality. I'm often surprised with what I get away with in terms of just being flippant with people. Then you become a little conscious of the fact that you've got a little bit of charm and then that's when you have to watch yourself. I feel the same way about my relationship with Twitter over the years. I started with Twitter in 2009 or 2010 when I was at the University of Cincinnati managing the lab there. I believe my first tweet was about some conference we were participating in. It was a mold-making conference we were doing in Cincinnati and I wanted to get the word out. Then I was like, "Oh, this is a way for me to connect with other people who know Grasshopper or know how to do CNC machining," because at the time that was an imported skill brought to me by visiting professors from University of Michigan's Taubman College. When I was in grad school, Karl Daubmann and Craig Borum came down to Cincinnati and that was my big introduction

to that world. Then it was lonely when you're doing it by yourself, plus you have no one to learn from, so the learning is really slow when you're isolated like that. Then I realized Twitter was a tool for connecting to that broader community. Then even before I came to New York I saw CASE popping up and Designalyze with Zach Downey before I had anything to do with it. Today I'm conscious of the fact that Twitter is a medium that also promotes your personal brand. I'm not going to lie and be like, "I'm just still innocently sharing knowledge and connecting with the community." It's like, "No, I know that is a way to make sure that I have a certain amount of visibility." Granted it's in an extremely bizarre and small sub-pocket of one industry, but still.

How important is it that Superusers find a way to communicate what they're doing? Is it their job, or somebody else's job, to do that? "It's part of our job," says Hiram Rodriguez, computational design group leader at Thornton Tomasetti:

Whoever is the computational designer should be able to clearly state what their role is and how we are solving geometry and data problems in the industry, and how we're coming out with these tools and develop new plug-ins. If you want to talk about that, you can clearly say, "Okay, so what's your role?" The role is to come up with noble ways of interacting with data from various platforms where we can rationalize that.

Collaborators

Collaboration is a critical part of practice for all industry players but especially for Superusers who are the rare combination of a specialist that is often integrated on a team. DLR Group's Ryan Cameron sums it up nicely when he says, "I'm interested in providing value to architecture – value created with better design through increased collaboration, new techniques, and time for reflection. Future designers will need all three if they strive to create a better world." Collaboration, techniques, and time: Is one more important than another? Ryan explains:

They're all dependent on one another. There's an order of operation that almost *has* to happen with these. It's the dewy kind of collaboration that happens between everybody. What are the best

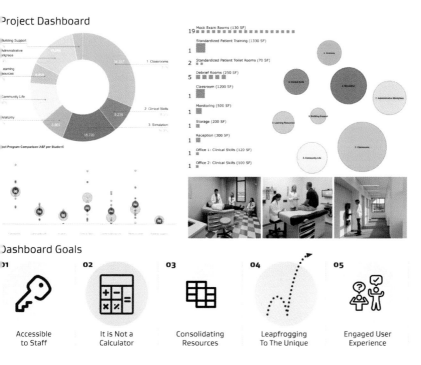

Figure 1.2
Web-based
dashboard to
visualize
project pro-
gram analy-
sis. (2018)
Credit: CO
Architects,
Robert
Canfield
Photography,
Frank
Oudeman.

techniques you've used to fish-out those best design ideas? You need to do this as quickly as you can to give your brain a chance to catch up with the speed that's out there now. That's the part that is the time for reflection. You really need all three. It's stepping back and describing the process as simply as possible. It's a bunch of people in a room, scrambling, mad, doing all kinds of sketches, or modeling, whatever the process is. It's enhanced by technology. We're still jotting ideas with pencils. We probably always will. Then, stepping back, we think "OK, we finished an 8-hour task in an hour. Let's take a moment to reflect on what we just did. Maybe what we just did isn't the best answer."

Firms struggle with promoting the idea that star employees, not teams, are behind the success of projects. Projects have become just too complex not to collaborate. For this reason and others, firms describe themselves as collaborative entities. "Over our history, LMN hasn't placed a lot of emphasis on self-promotion and in our office, there's no single star," says LMN Architects Principal Stephen Van Dyck:

There's no one person who's the author. We don't work that way. We make good on the idea of architecture as a collaborative endeavor, and that collaborative endeavor isn't just about the architects in our studio. Everyone we work with in the process plays an important part in the process. As architects we are all educated in school to believe that architects are the only part of the equation that matters. I sometimes feel like design awards reinforce this, implying that the architect is the reason that this is all happening. At LMN we have a general discomfort with that concept.

Van Dyck believes so much in the collaborative nature of practice that he was asked to pen the Foreword for Erin Carraher and Ryan E. Smith's book, *Leadership in Collaborative Architectural Practice*, about the fact that architecture now is no longer this top-down process. "It's much more collaboratively fostered, and there are systemic differences in how firms like ours work compared to other firms," says Van Dyck. "Their attempt in that book was to begin to codify that concept. It's no longer architect as genius. It's architect as orchestrator." Whether *leadership* in *collaborative* architectural practice is a contradiction in terms, the ability to collaborate with others is a critical capability that requires a collaborative mindset, one that the best Superusers deliberately practice.

Collaboration also has a place in the design technologist's toolbox, alongside virtual reality (VR.) "The key to everything is collaboration," says Ana Garcia Puyol, Director of User Experience and Integration at IrisVR:

Figure 1.3
**Superuser
model. (2018)
Credit:
Deutsch
Insights.**

So have everybody around. Gather everybody around the table. And to do that, you need a meeting. One of the key issues that we've seen is that VR might feel very isolating. And only by providing a way in which everyone can be in the VR meeting, then you're staying in the same space and you're not just looking at somebody with a headset on, but you're part of the conversation. You see their avatar, you can hear them. It's like a chat.

Garcia Puyol was trained in music and went to music school for 11 years. She was trained in classical music and studied piano on weekends for 6+ hours a day. She says:

It was insane. And my sister and I are twins. When we were 14 years old, we started learning jazz. And this was such a mind opening moment. We started learning improv and how to play blues. We would play together, four hands. One of us would do the bass or the bossa nova, and the other one would improvise at the top. And then we started playing in a big band. And there was a sense that there's a baseline, and then you get to do what you want.

There are few analogies more targeted to how Superusers work. As Garcia Puyol explains:

That's what I find so empowering about computational design, that you have to meet these goals, but hey, maybe this time we're going to use this two-by-four grid and then you know, there's this other option that might work a little bit better and it's using a grid that is three by six. The way I feel about design is that I just didn't want to be caged by the tools.

Working traditionally in architecture vs. having at your access emerging technologies, is the difference between playing classical and four-hand jazz piano. "If you do it the traditional way, you just do what's in front of you," she says. Garcia Puyol continues:

Whereas, if you learn certain technologies, then you're free to do whatever you want. So just put that into practice. And this is why this is not for everybody. Not because some people are not capable of doing it, but rather because their ambition, their philosophy, their take on things, they might be more comfortable doing just what is asked of them. There are a handful of people, not so many, that want to do more. They just feel like they want to be able to play a different tune.

That is why collaborating with others is a defining quality of Superusers.

Capacitors

As you'll sometimes hear Boomers and Gen-Xers tell it, if a project took four years from concept to realization, you worked on it for four years. That timeline's got to be harder for the current generation coming in. "Oh, yeah. I see it," says Hilda Espinal, CTO at CannonDesign "I see them getting excited about what's the newest, coolest thing, and running out of patience about always doing the same thing, all the time, for extended periods." Part of it is stick-with-it perseverance, some patience. But it is just as important that design technologists feel as though they have time – time to explore, time to inquire, time to search, and time even for downtime. A capacitor stores (electrical) energy and gives it off to the circuit when it's needed. Call this quality *capacity*: having the capacity to take on another assignment whether or not you actually have the time to do so. Having capacity means there is always time and energy, because you'll make it. A mindset, it's less about multitasking, which is seldom productive, than working smart.

"Architecture is at times like a puzzle where you have pieces but don't know their shapes yet," says Matthew Krissel, Partner at KieranTimberlake. He continues:

> The shapes emerge through a research, discovery, and exploration phase. They often slowly come into focus and even shift and change throughout design as things come together. We must remain open and flexible as we learn more about the place, people, their relationships, vision, and desires.

This ability to remain open, this agility with time, this abundance over scarcity mentality that is required to accomplish great work, this is *capacity*. As defined by Carol Dweck, it's the difference between having a fixed and growth mindset. Krissel continues:

I remember one of the first people I met when I came to Kieran-Timberlake was Richard Maimon, who incidentally is now one of my partners. We were working on a project together and when we completed a significant milestone, we talked about how we can all expect excellence from each other to do really good work, and it doesn't always have to be a linear relationship to time. An important lesson I learned early on was to become better at prioritizing the work and the importance of learning how to consistently do the right amount of work at the right time. Knowing when to unplug from a bad idea and how to not over-develop a concept in an iterative design process. Getting the right material at the right time, whether it's the tool you choose to use, your capacity to bring clarity at a time of uncertainty, or how much you model and simulate to make the pitch to move an idea forward matter. All these things impact our ability to be efficient with our time and impact others around us and their capacity to do great work ...

Obviously, no one hits every single attribute, especially people right out of school or new to the field, so you want to see their capacity to evolve and acquire these qualities.

Continual improvers

What is it about people like IrisVR's Ana Garcia Puyol, who upon discovering VR for the first time was so excited she stayed up all night dreaming up ways to apply it to architecture, whereas her sister, who introduced VR to Ana, didn't? "Through my architectural education I became a design thinker," explains Garcia Puyol. "So the moment my sister gave me a Google Cardboard and I put it onto my phone, it was like thinking about design. How design could be improved. How we could take things to the next level." This quality, to always strive to improve what already exists, is continual improvement, and the Superusers who have it are continual improvers. What makes someone a continual improver is having grit. Matthew Krissel explains:

Grit is a talent accelerant. It is taking talent and learning how to improve swiftly from mistakes, importance of persistence and

Figure 1.4
Diagram
describing
attributes of
KieranTim-
berlake's
digital design
platform is a
touchstone
for the group.
(2018) Credit:
KieranTim-
berlake.

Mission
Improve how we create knowledge, iterate
ideas, synthesize information, design, build,
and communicate our work.

Who
A collective of people,
processes, and technology
accountable for shaping and
extending digital design
practices across the firm and
the broader profession.

Our central obligation is to
ensure ample time, flexibility,
and resources to explore ideas,
tools, and workflows, and
transfer knowledge to all
individuals.

**How might
digital design
expand our creative
potential, discover
new opportunities,
and amplify our
ability to deliver
exemplary
projects?**

What
A forum for scrutinizing ou
industry and identifying
emerging needs and
opportunities for change.

Expand our capacity to
evolve and speculate on
technological advancemen
in our industry.

Raise discourse about nea
and long-term aspirations
our practice of architectur

Why
Take responsibility as designers to
solve the great challenges of our time.

Couple data with intuition,
combinatorial thinking, and digital
tools to see, retain, communicate, and
synthesize more.

Find new connections between
disparate ideas and generate new
insight into problems.

Drive emergent technology to design
and deliver work that elevates the
human experience.

How
Perpetually practice, engage, and
thrive within the knowledge
structures of data, information,
and virtual/physical experiences.

Promote the value of
experimentation and the virtue
of failing forward.

Persist in developing new and
creative ways to work in an open
marketplace of ideas.

working iteratively and the value of enjoying the churn and
challenge of continuous improvement. Good design is hard –
you have to be persistent and enjoy that persistence.

Concentrators

Even with the distractions of contemporary work-life, Superusers are
able to focus. They see failure as part of the process, but when they
do fail, they fail fast – and fail forward. They don't waste time on
dead-ends, chasing unpromising schemes. In this sense, the work
they do is "concentrated" and they are concentrators. NBBJ's Dan
Anthony captures the concentrator's ability perfectly when he says
all effective design technologists share one quality, "To do the hard
thing once instead of doing the easy thing a thousand times." That's
a concentrator.

Too much in design is left to chance, leaving the owner – and
often the firm – with risk. There's too much unknown and at stake.

Architects may be comfortable with ambiguity, while owners want clarity and certainty. Superusers are able to focus on, and interpret, what they are working on in terms of going from uncertainty to certainty, ambiguity to clarity; complexity to simplicity, and time-intensive to instantaneous and immediate.

Computational thinkers

To be able to use computational tools is a skillset, and to think computationally is a mindset. It means to ask, when confronted with a wicked (intractable, not easy to solve) problem: is this a problem that could benefit from automation, from computation? It doesn't mean you're a hammer seeing every problem as a nail. When Jordan Billingsley first started at Hord Coplan Macht, computational tools weren't being used at all. "The BIM gurus and BIM power users, they were all aware of Dynamo, but nobody felt like they had the time to learn it," says Billingsley. He continues:

> When I came on I hadn't used Dynamo either, but I kept getting these issues, and as I was documenting them I kept coming across Dynamo solutions, so I started working on Dynamo graphs, and shortly afterwards we hired someone who had used a lot of Dynamo in their grad school program and had some Python experience. He's been taking that on as a leader so I don't have to be as involved with learning the stuff, and I can start doing more recruiting of people and training to get people excited about it. Because what we're trying to train people about is not how to use Grasshopper, not how to use Dynamo, it's about how to think computationally, how to recognize when to ask, "Is this something we can automate?"

Automating processes is associated with deskilling of design tasks, sometimes seen as threatening to design professionals, that they will be automated out of a job. Others, like LMN Architects Principal Stephen Van Dyck, see automating as an opportunity in that it frees designers to think, including thinking computationally. "To me in that context, 'skilling' is just labor," explains Van Dyck. He continues:

> Nobody likes to labor, everybody likes thinking. We're trying to do less labor, more thinking. That's what new technologies are allowing us to do …

Of course, today, I'm pretty far off the curve of capability with these tools. In fact, I wouldn't ever say that I was an advanced user of any technology. I just happened to know enough to be dangerous. That's actually an important thing I would tell students. Then, you've got to say, "Okay, who else has this knowledge out there that I can collaborate with?" And if you don't have these tools in hand, or people in the office with the corresponding skillset, maybe you need to make investments. Attract and educate for new skills to enable the implementation of new ways of working.

Over the years, Thornton Tomasetti's Hiram Rodriguez has grown to look at problems from a computation perspective. He says:

This allows me to know what paths and how much time it will take to deliver a coherent scheme for a particular project. The key part here is that we can show that by using a set of tools we can save X amount of time and we can deliver not only one scheme but maybe we have 2 more options to show our client. So that's a valuable thing that we bring into the industry and I can bring that into the project team and say, "Okay, well, here's the base scheme, but because I have these tools, here is this other scheme."

Coders

The preceding nine qualities are considered mindsets or soft skills. There's no way around it, the final attribute is a skillset: *coding*. Superusers are coders. Some are undoubtedly more advanced than others, some have more opportunities to lift the hood on the software they are using, but Superusers must be fearless in their pursuit of taking tool destiny into their own hands. A whole book could be written on coding – Amazon shows over 10,000 results for a coding books' search – here we'll try to sum up this final Superusers' distinguishing characteristic.

On the one extreme are the software developers who are hired to code. Shane Burger explains:

When I am looking at hiring people within my own team, which serves more of a role as consulting specialists, there are two groups. One group is core software developers. I'm hiring for that position now. In the case of a core software developer some

Figure 1.5
CannonDe-
sign Yazdani
Studio 2.
(2018) Credit:
Yazdani
Studio of
CannonDe-
sign.

of the soft skills are a little less important. But they do need to be able to work with the team.

Tool maker is a skill but can also be seen as a mindset. He continues:

In the many years I have been involved in computation, going back to the first SmartGeometry, the designer's a tool builder. And the designer is a person who can create their own design space. That hasn't changed. It keeps going. It keeps developing. We're seeing students and graduates out of the university coming with that as a default mindset. It's fantastic that they're continuing to do it. There is a lot more hands-on engagement today, which is good.

On the other extreme are the busy design technology leaders who, day-in day-out, don't get to code and long for the opportunity to code more. When NBBJ's Dan Anthony was asked, "If you could spend your time doing anything, what would you do?" He responded, "Frankly, I would love to be coding more," and explained:

I know that sounds crazy. I often find that I am thinking: if I only had two more hours we could turn this from something that is just project-specific to something that could impact the next project. And I do that sometimes.

Coding can be leveraged for customizing tools and speeding-up processes. One example is where NBBJ recently built an easy technique for finding views from Revit that match Google Earth perspectives. Anthony explains:

So we can get a real-world view of the space. There are other softwares that do this, but we wanted to make it happen quickly for our team. Again, if I had a little more time, I'd automatically bring that view into Revit. Then it would be right there. Or maybe drop it into a VR environment.

Being able to code is seen as a basic, inalienable skillset by many design technologists. "We had architecture students from Iowa State come through DLR Group's Des Moines office the other day," says Ryan Cameron:

They asked, "If there's one thing that we need to learn, what is it?" I said: "If you can't code, I'm probably not going to hire you." I was going to take it back right away, but I stuck with it. I'm going to let this sit and settle a little bit and see if it dissolves or not. I'm glad I did wait because, not only did the chaperone say, "yes, I've heard that too," and all of the students nodded their heads: "*Yeah, I keep hearing that. That we should learn coding.*" I responded to them, I'm not expecting you to be a computer programmer and architect at the same time. But, having a basic understanding of how that system works – maybe they won't use it for design – but people can take advantage of you if you don't have this understanding, an ability to code and program. If you can do it yourself, you're going to save a lot of time and money. That's what it comes down to. I've been coding things myself. I'll think, this is a $3000 software and I could basically rebuild the parts that I need from it for a hundred bucks.

Not having the ability to code and program puts you at the mercy of software manufacturers. If you can't go under the hood and customize the product out-of-the-box, making the tool more accessible or do what you really need for it to do, it "puts you at a strategic disadvantage," says Cameron. As for existing tools, "They are there to help provide a solid foundation for you to build off of but they can't customize every unique button you want it to do," explains Cameron.

To be sure, not every Superuser has all ten C-factors, or for those that do, not all are likely at the same level of development. Refer frequently to these competencies, qualities, and attributes – mindsets and skillsets – to identify areas for improvement.

An eleventh C?

There are undoubtedly additional qualities, or even Cs, that one could add to this list. "Sometimes they have a crowd," suggests Ryan Cameron. "Just by being next to that person they will absorb knowledge or be more creative. Having a crowd gives you more opportunity for feedback, which is critical in design technology."

These qualities help distinguish Superusers from run-of-the-mill technology specialists. The next chapter will look at specific Superuser superpowers – capabilities that make Superusers so valuable to the success of firms.

Chapter 2

Superuser superpowers

"They see me write this script that basically takes a click in Excel and modifies the entire Dynamo file, color codes it, then spits out a report in Microsoft Power BI and a Revit model, all simultaneously," says Ryan Cameron, Project Architect at DLR Group. "It's a whole cost-estimating, data-driven decision-making program. We used it in an interview here and won a project in the Midwest." Cameron explains how this was accomplished:

> We gave the remote mouse to the client: pick your options in the Excel drop-down and hit save. It was all color-coded so Option A was red; Option B was blue; Option C was green. Their programming needed to be a B-grade option. Their corridors needed to be a C-grade option, and so on. They saved it and could instantly visualize the decision they made at the interview level. All the colors changed in the 3D model. The Revit model updated with all new cost information and all of that exported to the Power BI dashboard that was up on the second screen. We hit refresh. That decision, just did all of this. We ended up getting the project: Writing a little script – even a pretty big script – was absolutely a contributing factor to why we got it.

Cameron added, "The best part was it being used by someone who has no idea what they are doing. That was my goal."

Building your team

This story illustrates certain "tells" in a candidate or design professional that makes them stand apart. Their ability to code certainly helps, and so does already having an existing relationship with the client, which, according to Cameron, probably weighed in just as much as writing a script that could instantaneously accomplish all of what it did. But what also needs to be weighed in is the design technologist's ability to ferret out what is important to clients, what will win them over, and to get clients – who do not normally work with these tools – to experience the tools and process themselves. This ability – and a small number of others that will be covered in this chapter – are Superusers' differentiators: their *superpowers*. Scripting code is still not a common skill among architects and other design professionals. "My research suggests that the majority of the industry probably can't script it," says Cameron, "that's OK for now."

Superuser superpowers are the things you look for in the people who are going to work on your team. What are the soft skills, mindsets, and attitudes that firm leaders look for in individuals? According to Principal Shane Burger:

> There are a couple different tiers within Woods Bagot. There are people who I'm trying to help advise, to move onto projects, and to be embedded within projects. They'll be on that project full time except for the fact that they have additional skills that they can bring to the team that others may not have.
>
> When I am looking at hiring people within my own team, which serves more of a role as consulting specialists, there are two groups. One group is core software developers. I'm hiring for that position now. In the case of a core software developer some of the soft skills are a little less important. But they do need to be able to work with the team. Yet they need not be client-facing. When I say "client," I'm not necessarily referring to external clients. I'm often referring to internal clients.

To be client-facing, irrespective of whom the client may be, design technologists need interpersonal skills.

Ten Superuser superpowers

Ten Superuser superpowers cover problem-solving and communication skills, interpersonal and conversational skills, question-asking, thought leadership, and storytelling. This chapter looks at these and other qualities firm leaders look for when identifying people for their

Figure 2.1
Timeline of
CO Archi-
tects' tech-
nology imple-
mentation
and represen-
tative pro-
jects. (2018)
Credit: CO
Architects,
Timothy
Hursley, Tom
Bonner
Photography,
Assassi Pro-
ductions,
Robert
Canfield
Photography,
Timmerman
Photography,
Jeremy
Bittermann
Photography,
Frank
Oudeman.

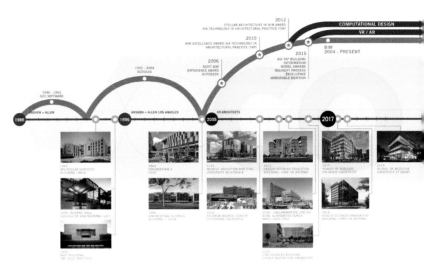

teams. Among these are the most often-mentioned superpower, teachability, or a thirst for learning; and, not applying computational processes, but how to think computationally, identify repeatable tasks, and recognize when to ask, "Is this something we can automate?" This chapter also looks at possessing an entrepreneurial spirit, and how Superusers strive to contribute to something bigger beyond the task at hand. Finally, the chapter ends with the intangibles – those hard-to-define qualities that all design technology specialists share and their employers recognize, value, and reward – and looks at Superusers as 5-tool players in architecture and as force multipliers in their firms.

Interpersonal skills

What are some of the special challenges of leading design technologists – who are, by and large, tech-types? Are design technologists more or less easily bored than other employees? More or less utilized than other employees? Burger says:

> This speaks to my desire to find the right personality types for hiring problem solvers. Perhaps because of this focus I run into fewer of these problems. I do have members of my team that fit in this category. It mostly has to do with getting them to engage socially, verbally, and talking with people. Getting out there. I didn't have this problem with Brian Ringley or Andrew Heumann because their

names were known across the practice. Everybody knew who they were because they were personalities that got out there and talked to people. But I have other members of my team where, just in their last performance review, I had to push them and say, listen, for me to keep being able to feed you some of the best projects, it benefits me and it benefits you for people to know who you are

In terms of career path, one of our qualifications when it comes to advancement in the company is that you're respected by your peers. You cannot be respected by your peers if nobody knows who you are. This can run against some of the personalities of some of the people to do this. They're not about self-promotion – and I'm not even talking about self-promotion. I am talking about some better interpersonal skills in terms of how you engage with people.

Sometimes, as technology leaders, we think about the people that work with us as being do-it-yourselfers (DIYers) as opposed to being collaborative or working in teams. Which do firm leaders count on to get the job done? According to Hilda Espinal, CTO at CannonDesign:

It's more of the latter. Yes, you hold on to specialists for certain things. But, that specialty has an expiration date. So then what are you going to do? You have to be able to be flexible. You have to be able to become collaborative.

Collaboration – one of the ten Cs from the previous chapter – requires interpersonal skills to flourish.

Over time, Espinal has brought in over 40 professionals into the Digital Practice and Practice Technology Teams at various firms where she formed these teams. She says:

Every single time that I talked to them about how things are going, at performance review time, almost always they would say, "You know what I love about our team is that I don't have all the answers, but I know to call this other person on the west coast and ask him, or this gal on the east coast" . . .

So, there's a crosspollination of expertise and there's a lot to be learned by having this collaborative environment. Working in silos, that's the ultimate definition of knowledge-is-power. Forget that. That's not the way.

You need to do your stuff well, you have to be able to contribute, and perhaps you know something that others don't and that's the specialization part. But, the rest of it, you have to be collaborative and work with others. It's like interoperability.

To do this, design technologists need conversational skills.

Conversational skills

Related to interpersonal skills is the ability to speak and engage in conversation with others. Shane Burger says:

A lot of people have this idea that computational designers put their heads down, they're very code-heavy, and can't really talk to others – having the ability to speak, especially with lead designers, is really important.

You have to get them to buy into a change in methodology. Not just the use of software for the change in methodology. It involves good conversational skills, to talk people into it. To get them to buy into the process, they have to think of you, affectively, as at their level. Not as, here's my Grasshopper guy who's going to go off and do this for me. Or, here's my guy who's going to write a VR app for me. They have to feel like they are talking to a peer. That's really important.

I can interview people who are absolutely amazing in terms of their computational skills, scripting skills, or whatever. But I have

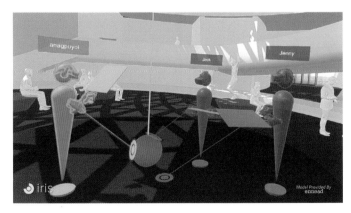

Figure 2.2
Ennead
Shanghai Pla-
netarium
multiuser
meeting in
first-person
mode as seen
in IrisVR Pro-
spect. AGP.
(2018) Credit:
IrisVR, Ana
Garcia Puyol,
Ennead
Architects.

to give a bit of a pause if I also didn't feel comfortable talking with them.

Problem identifying and solving

If someone were to ask him what his most valuable ability is, DLR Group's Ryan Cameron would tell you it would be problem solving. He's not alone in this assessment. "For the core team, probably the most important soft skill is just being a problem solver," says Shane Burger. "Wanting to dig in to a problem the moment they see it. It's that sort of personality that trumps any need, in some cases for actually having the technical skills. Because you'll figure it out." Burger continues:

> The example for me is even thinking back to working with Brian Ringley for so long. Brian did not have all the skills he needed when he started. But he was absolutely engaged, and was a huge problem-solver. He picked up a tremendous amount during his time here. So, that's more important to me: a person who is a problem-solver.

Being the first able to identify the problems worth solving is a bonus skill.

Entrepreneurialism

An entrepreneurial spirit can carry through from outside work experiences into one's current role as design technologist. During Jordan Billingsley's undergraduate years he started a small business, Blackline Supply, with a mission to serve his fellow architecture students. While running this business, he worked for Porter Athletic and then the Army Corps of Engineers at the Construction Engineering Research Laboratory (CERL). At Porter Athletic he learned how to create complex parametric Revit families and at CERL how to build Excel-based calculators off information databases. "Job prospects were bleak when I graduated but Blackline had proven itself to be a valuable resource to students so I decided to double down on my entrepreneurial efforts and began freelancing prototyping and rendering services to professionals," says Billingsley, now a design technology specialist with Hord Coplan Macht. He continues:

Blackline became sort of a half-way house for graduates in similar situations to work on their portfolio and enter competitions while searching for full time employment. It was a very rewarding experience but I never viewed Blackline as something to capitalize on financially. When I got married I encouraged my wife to accept a position at Johns Hopkins University and I handed off business operations to a group of students. I then began a search for my first job at an architecture firm and was very blessed to land a position with Hord Coplan Macht as their BIM Coordinator where my entrepreneurial spirit has been supported to take on new and evolving responsibilities, including leading their Design Technology group.

This entrepreneurial attitude can carry through to one's project work. "At Thornton Tomasetti (TT), we were all architects who knew how to code and make proof of concepts," says Ana Garcia Puyol, Director of User Experience and Integration at IrisVR. "If VRX was an actual company like IrisVR is, perhaps we would've hired programmers who could leverage VR to work with structural engineering workflows." Garcia Puyol is an example of someone who left an AE firm to work for a startup, as is Jonatan Schumacher, to head-up Konstru, and now at WeWork. Someone at TT came up with Konstru because either somebody was doing it in another industry and they needed to do it in ours, or somebody was doing it but TT didn't have a version that was interoperable with the tools we're using. It's that kind of mindset, an entrepreneurial mindset, where someone like Schumacher thinks, *Wait a second, Konstru (or Reconstruct, Flux, or whatever) will really connect all the dots*. This superpower is the entrepreneurial mindset.

Contributing to something bigger

Jaron Lanier, the computer philosophy writer and computer scientist, when asked what his best VR experience has ever been, said it's when he takes the headset off and experiences real life: the subtle things like breezes that you can't replicate in VR.[1] When IrisVR's Ana Garcia Puyol was asked what her favorite part of this tech job was, she responded, "Oh, it's definitely working with people. It's visiting firms, interacting with them." In the world of VR literature, that's becoming a pattern. Almost as though the technology makes us appreciate people, collaboration, interaction more. Garcia Puyol explains:

For me, that has less to do with the fact that I work in VR and more in general with how I feel about helping other people and making sure that what I do contributes to something bigger than me coming to the office and making sketches or designing something or even punching some code on the screen.

So, does she find her work in design technology to be more meaningful than just focusing on an object or product or a building? She says:

Yeah, I like the idea of contributing to something bigger than what I'm trying to accomplish at the end of the day, that I can help others. Even when I've taught in the past, I try to make an effort to reach out to women, especially to younger women. Because I feel like my particular skills might not be something that women think of as a career opportunity. I feel strongly about that. I have a responsibility in that sense and I want to make sure that if I can do something, I might as well do it for the improvement of the workflow, of the way in which people work.

Teachability

The most often-mentioned superpower is an obsession with learning, with gaining knowledge. Shane Burger mentioned that a primary quality he looks for in a team member is a person who is a problem-solver. What comes next? "Secondarily, [is] a thirst for learning," says Burger. "Never feeling satisfied with where they are. Wanting always to learn

Figure 2.3
Ennead
Shanghai Pla-
netarium
multiuser
meeting in
first-person
mode as seen
in IrisVR Pro-
spect. (2018)
Credit: IrisVR,
Ana Garcia
Puyol,
Ennead
Architects.

the next thing, and extend themselves even further." As these super-powers are all interrelated, one's ability to work well on teams, and well-developed conversational and interpersonal skills, are co-related with a desire to learn. Coupled with teachability is a thirst for knowledge, "focused around our specific profession and obtaining as much knowledge as quickly as you can to do great things," says Ryan Cameron.

Burger says:

Someone can have amazing technical skills, and know all the things in the world about how to code in C#, but not be good working in a team. That is actually more of a problem. They can always pick up better coding skills. They can always pick up new languages. They can always learn new ways of dealing with geometry, analysis, or whatever. But having the right mindset, and the desire to learn, is actually a much bigger thing. What I don't want is someone who can't talk to others, and sits back on their hands saying to themselves *I already know this.* That's no good.

CannonDesign's CTO Hilda Espinal agrees. "How much do you know about where to find this button or how to write this script, all that can be taught," says Espinal. "I'm not worried about that. You must have some foundation, you've got to at least hit the ground walking, maybe not running, but the rest of it? It's learnable. I'm not so worried about it."

Fail fast, fail forward

Many architects – including emerging professionals and those just out of school – see themselves as perfectionists. Design technology often requires trial and error, and experimentation. Perfectionism could be seen as a challenge to a design technologist's experimental approach. One of the ways firm leaders might suggest this be overcome is by taking a fail fast attitude.

As an antidote to perfectionism, KieranTimberlake has a fail fast approach, ethos, and attitude. "We know that the path to making exceptional work is not always clear, mistakes will happen, and the process may get messy," says partner Matthew Krissel. "But those kinds of setbacks are essential to creating great work. That's why we constantly question ourselves, our practices, and remain open to change." And failing is part of that process, especially in the design phase, when things are still digital, before construction. "If you are not failing at times, then you are not pushing yourself or ever going to reach your potential," adds Krissel. "Success is wonderful, but it can unfortunately lull people into doing the same thing over and over. Mistakes however, promote growth and change and hone our ability to be nimble, reflective, and learn to course correct."

Krissel discusses failure as a necessary part of the design process, and as with the other superpowers, tied in with continuous learning:

> If people are open minded I believe in the right environment they can learn to become comfortable with failing forward. This is not about accepting sub-optimal work and of course repeated mistakes where change and learning are not occurring is not acceptable. Instead of an abstract notion of perfection, focus on striving for excellence in everything you do. This pursuit can only be achieved if you are continuously learning and if you leverage and work with other people around you to overcome your weaknesses. Recognizing this not as a fault but a virtue that will build resourcefulness, growth, and your capacity to design your relationships well.

Thought leadership

Knowledge sharing is a big part of what design technologists do, and to do that consistently, and effectively, they need to be socially skilled. I asked Ryan Cameron if there was a better name than *Superuser* to describe socially adept design technologists? "A thought leader comes to mind," he replied, continuing, "a liaison who – if they can't do the work themselves – they know who to reach out to, or where to reach, to get that goal accomplished." Thought leader is a title that he has been recognized with by his firm, in part from work he has done through their professional development grant (PDG) program. "The PDG awards winners 80 hours of extra paid time off plus up to $5,000 to pursue a passion project," Cameron explains. He continues:

> In 2015, for me and my colleague Michael Vander Ploeg, that project was Data Streams. That ended up turning into a product – which led to another research endeavor. In 2016, a young

employee named Liz, from our Phoenix office, put together a collection of members of the firm who were providing some thought leadership value. I was one of the four mentioned in her presentation to DLR Group's executive team. I thought that was good, fun, and interesting. I was also involved in the 2017 PDG program through a contribution to another project, a series of digital books capturing design culture at DLR Group led by Jill and Dillon from our Seattle office. Knowledge sharing is a trait of some of the most successful people in DLR Group, and it's a great model for myself and others in the firm.

Why might someone scoff at the title "design technologists"? Could it be that design technologists represent more than just a bunch of people experimenting with technology? Cameron says:

That's how it gets perceived sometimes. You get these people with a phenomenal understanding of their tools, but they reached a higher level in terms of how to build a community, how to distribute tools, and how to help people learn. So, it goes beyond design technology.

Some of the more familiar design technologists had built a name for themselves and, in doing so, a following. Burger explains:

Over time, I developed great appreciation for the people that I worked with, that were also challenging the profession. From a big picture perspective.

Basically, what we're saying is that what we're doing as a profession isn't enough, so let's do something better. That goes beyond trying to challenge yourself, within the practice, to do something newer and better than a project. It's now saying, actually reaching out to the industry at large is an important part of that. That gets into public speaking engagements. That gets into public debates. Really having a well-developed, informed opinion. Their critical thinking skills become key for this.

Design technology is filled with people who are more comfortable sitting in front of a monitor than engaging with people. Are these more familiar design technologists, who built a name and a following, more gregarious and outgoing than the average design technologist? NBBJ's Dan Anthony says:

It's complicated. Mostly, I am interested in the relationships that help form these kinds of environments that lead to the most productive and interesting activities. I definitely recognize that I toe both lines. I'd say that at times I am more gregarious than I am effective. But I think it's really important to have both qualities. I practice communication as a way to transmit knowledge.

One of Anthony's hobbies has been acting and performance. At Stanford he ran the Shakespeare group for a couple years. Anthony admits:

Part of that is that I am not the best actor – I can never remember my lines. But I was really interested in the way that we used language to communicate ideas. I had a lot of friends who I really admired who were good at it. Whom I wanted to support in the work they did. I've always been involved in that. To me, that's a really important part. All of this knowledge isn't useful if you can't communicate about it, if you can't share it. It's a weird skill because it may take you out of being the guy in the cubicle.

Storytelling

Storytelling goes hand-in-hand with thought leadership. Part of IrisVR's Ana Garcia Puyol's role with integration and user experience is leveraging her architectural experience where she is able to interpret either metaphorically or directly how a designer or architect might leverage the tool. Garcia Puyol explains:

I tell the team a lot about storytelling. Even in structural design, there is a lot of storytelling. Because you can make the distance between columns larger but then you're going to have beefier columns, or you're going to have to spend more money in another system that allows for those columns to be thinner. So there's a story to be told, of what this building says to the people who see and experience it. That's what I try to convey to the team.

Through a combination of her education, talent, and exposure to design thinking, Garcia Puyol considers what she does at IrisVR as *storytelling through technology.* "I always put it this way: 'Architects don't make homes, they make happy families.' The architect gets to tell us the story of a better future, one that they get to build," explains Garcia Puyol. "I wanted to be part of a generation that helps other professionals make that happen, to shape these ideas, those dreams."

LMN Architects Principal Stephen Van Dyck believes architects must be able to tell a compelling story. "That's what we do, right? We tell stories to people to discover and explain good ideas that somebody else might want to pay for," says Van Dyck. He continues:

That's the part of architecture that I have gravitated towards. I studied architecture history, which is essentially the creation of stories. In college, I took this class called The Histories of Architecture, before which I remember expecting that it would just be a lot of stories about architecture, and that they're all going to line up in some neat way. But no, it was in fact about all the different stories about architecture, different narratives that were created out of the same sets of evidence.

To Van Dyck, telling stories about architecture was just as much an interesting and fun puzzle to solve as designing a building. Van Dyck asks:

How do we tell the stories of ideas to our clients? How do we tell our story as a firm? How do we tell our story as people who see promise in technology? How do we tell our story to our peers and the academy, to help see what we can add to the dialogue in the academic world?

Figure 2.4 Designers have long utilized different perspectives to describe architectural space. VR/AR improves upon those views by expanding the range of views, allowing viewers to quickly toggle back and forth between views. (2018) Credit: CO Architects.

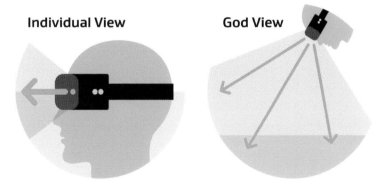

Individual View   God View

Question-asking

How important is asking penetrating, insightful questions in the work of design technologists? Is question-asking a quality employers look for and value? And how do Superusers become better question-askers? Matthew Krissel says:

> It's a skill you get better at. You may have the instinct, or you will have to cultivate it, but it is something you get better at it as you practice and mature. It's not just asking questions but using inquiry as a design tool to bring clarity and help other people around you engage and advance the conversation.

Expanding on the notion of inquiry as a design tool, Krissel adds:

> It is essential to understand the complexity and interconnectivity of people and the built environment to do transformative design work. Therefore, asking a good question is vital in a design practice. It is important to see design as a liquid and not a solid. Design is not a destination but a process of becoming.

KieranTimberlake is often asked to design something for which it is not an expert. "How are we going to learn all this?" asks Krissel. "We ask good questions, we listen, observe, and iterate. A great question is generative and helps one from falling into complacent patterns and ideation echo chambers." Elaborating, Krissel adds:

> Too often I see designers with a solution looking for a problem and they cram a diagram through the process. As architects and designers, we are service providers and often the problem someone comes to you with may not be well formed. It is critical to ensure we have defined what and why we are designing something. You must forget everything you know about a subject so that you can approach a problem with clarity, objectivity and be prepared to go deep and iterate. This why we consistently organize ourselves around the things that we don't know and not knowing can be a valuable position to be in as it lets us be impartial and open to change or new ideas. So how then does one ask better questions? A good question needs to challenge assumptions and seek clarity. It should help one understand

short-term and long-term implications, engage others in ideation and often reframe the discussion.

At a higher level, it is important to understand the *question behind the question* that is being asked. "My mantra has always been *everything that we do needs to be purpose-built*. That's not just tools," says Cory Brugger, Director of Technology at Morphosis from 2010–2017, and now CTO of HKS. He continues:

> When you're building an architectural design model you need to ask yourself and your team; where are we in the design process? What do we need to answer? Is this viable? Does this detail work? Does the material work? You're only building something to answer design questions, what or why, at any given moment. That's where the evolution comes in. Part of it is taking a step back and saying, why are we going to do this next step? Why are we going to prototype something? Why are we building a tool? What will we get out of it? We don't want to build technology for the sake of technology, especially when it may not be a technology problem.

Intangibles

The last of the ten Superuser superpowers are *intangibles*, abilities that go beyond that which can be fully explained, sussed out, or grasped. They include drive, and ability to prioritize, an ability to think in 3D, personality, and an inclination to teach.

Drive

Superusers are *driven* to do what they do. They aren't motivated extrinsically by gift cards or attaboys or attagirls. According to Shane Burger:

> Probably the single biggest challenge I've run into in the traditional *leading geeks* group, is building up a certain level of drive within them, so I don't have to be the person to constantly facilitate conversation.
>
> They can get out there and do it themselves. And it's a benefit if they learn to do it themselves. I'm not a manager where I need

to have everything go through me. In fact, the more and more I begin to trust you, the less I need to be aware of what's happening there. I trust that these people will elevate problems as they need to be. I'm constantly in that position where I'm like, no, just call them on the phone, and let's talk about it. Or, step number one is to reach out to people and ask them what they want. Build up requirements that way. To get them to be outside of their bubble is probably one of the more difficult things.

Ability to prioritize

Can design technologists experience work-life balance if they're reading 50 blogs, doing tutorials, staying on their toes, and preparing for the next meeting? "A lot of people would say that the only way to maintain work-life balance is for your work to become your life and your life to become your work," explains Jordan Billingsley. He continues:

> But I believe that the more you talk about things, the clearer things are in your head, the more you're able to talk out loud. Then you start to recognize patterns and are able to talk about these topics so fluidly. Once you become adept at identifying these patterns it is actually quite easy to scan 50 blogs in my Feedly. It takes me about 20–40 seconds to determine if a blog post is novel and warrants in-depth reading. Over time you get a good sense of what is important … This ability to discern, to zero-in or cut bait, requires detachment, to determine something's ultimate value.

Ability to think in 3D

What do computational designers do differently and even *better* – faster, smarter – than traditional architects or structural engineers? What's their differentiating superpower? What do they bring to their job beside curiosity? One such superpower acquired over time is an ability to think in multiple dimensions. Hiram Rodriguez, computational design group leader at Thornton Tomasetti, says:

> One thing that I noticed about myself being in this role and with TT, is that I can comprehend a problem in 3D better than most of my

49

colleagues and also use my skills to think about what would be the best workflow for a particular problem.

Working with all practices within the company has given me a better understanding of technology within the AEC industry, thus I can rationalize potential paths for a specific problem. That is something that not a lot people have.

Superusers as force multipliers

Krissel says:

I see a Superuser as a force multiplier. While they are often associated with tool proficiency, it also touches on the importance of soft skills and the ability to make others around you better. The ability to constructively reframe a problem, read between the lines, recognize patterns while listening and observing. They tend to be optimistic, "We over me," and nimbler then most. Their elastic mind consistently turns constraints into opportunities and they are rarely phased by uncertainty. They are proactive in designing their habits, relationships, and workflows. They also tend to have an entrepreneurial streak in the way they are always seeking new problems to solve.

Figure 2.5
Superusers, as force multipliers, make everybody around them better. (2018) Credit: Deutsch Insights.

Krissel admits that ultimately no one is good at everything, "but Superusers are people who know what they can and cannot do and they orchestrate teams around them with the right people, processes, and technology to overcome weaknesses and amplify strengths to levels not achievable alone."

Personality

One superpower, comfort with the people side of things, enables Superusers to work on more interesting assignments or opportunities to work with interesting people. "I've definitely struck up a lot of professional friendships that have led to opportunities," says WeWork Senior Researcher Brian Ringley. He continues:

> I'm sure that personality is a big part of that. I was actually told by Marc Swackhamer, one of my freshman year design professors, and remember him telling me – we were having a cookout at his house at the end of the year – that my biggest asset was my sense of humor and that would actually take me far in the industry. Those words really rang true.

On the role emotions play in one's career, Ringley added:

> At the same time, I'm still consciously trying to be nice and fun to be around because it's stressful to deliver projects, and people who can control their emotions if you have to put in that late night and somebody's mad at you, or money is draining out of the project coffers because there are delays, all the various crises that erupt in a project. If you can maintain your composure and be fun to be around, then it's just going to be better for everyone. I'm still consciously cultivating that, because I definitely break down and get grumpy, and get stressed out and snap at people and that's never been productive, so that's something I'm still constantly working on.

In the AEC industry, architects, especially engineers, tend to be introverts. If you're an extrovert in our industry, you can go really far. Some design professionals, like myself, are *ambiverts* – when around introverted people they become extroverted and vice versa. How important is it to be a people person when working with design technology? Garcia Puyol admits:

> My entire life I thought I was an extrovert, that I was very comfortable with people. But then in the past few years, particularly in New York, I realized how much time I spend on my own. And because of music school and then architecture school, even though you're working with people, you spend a lot of time in your head. Getting things done. I read a ton, as much as I can. Many Fridays, I get home and I turn off my phone until Saturday morning. Then I can reach out to my friends again and hang out over the weekend. I enjoy more and more giving presentations and talking to people. With women, trying to reach out and serve as a role model for them, so they can think, "Oh, this is something I can be doing too." So yeah, it's funny, maybe I'm an ambivert. I've been reading about it recently too. Maybe that's a good combination so that you can convey your ideas to other people, try to make it clear to others and then for those ideas to have a grounding, you need your own space. I need to write ideas down, and let them sit for a little bit and then pick them up later. And those things need to happen when I'm on my own. There's no way they can happen with people around me.

One's personality can have an impact on their energy levels. It has been a revelation for people to discover in recent years, for example, that introverts are actually exhausted by people. Garcia Puyol says:

> For me, it's been mainly about accepting that. That's okay. Maybe on my Friday evening, I need my energy and then I can enjoy my weekend again with my friends. Work takes a lot of oneself. I have a job that is similar to when I was in architecture school, very creative. So it's very crazy but at the same time, I talk to my colleagues about it, and we all agree, we get to make these new workflows up and that takes so much energy. And that's okay. To me it's OK just to make peace with it. So maybe when I get home it's okay that I just rest because we just did this thing that doesn't exist.

An inclination to teach

To be a Superuser, design technologists need to be good at teaching. Shane Burger explains:

The teaching part is important to me because, the way I structured the teams at Woods Bagot, is to never have a project team develop a dependency on a consulting specialist. The point of that is I always want to partner-up one of my team members with someone in a project team or studio to learn from what's happening. This way, the person on my team doesn't have to keep doing the same thing again and again. They off-load knowledge. They teach others. Through that process, they build-up the skill sets throughout the whole company. This is where social skills become really important. About how well you can teach others.

Thornton Tomasetti's Hiram Rodriguez is a great example of a Superuser who teaches on the job. He says:

There's an interest within the company to understand what parametric design is and we're pushing that forward. Our group is trying to put information out there for everybody and we try to make presentations every month. That is one of my tasks. I try to gather people around, teach them about what computational design is, because you need to understand what computational design is in order to ask the right questions. It is important to have your staff informed about what it means to use Grasshopper or other visual programming tools, it allows them to understand what would be the best time to use a tool.

Superusers as 5-tool players in architecture
KieranTimberlake's Matthew Krissel likens Superusers to 5-tool players in baseball – someone who hits for power, average, fields, throws, and runs:

In architecture, it's a person who can Design (creative, big picture, as well as the details, can synthesize, productively curious), Communicate (speak with clarity, thoughtful visualization, presentations, good collaborator, knowledge sharing), Research (ask good questions, good with data, objective, observant, an explorer), [be a] Tool Agnostic (right tool at the right time, always learning, continuously improving), [and have a good] Work-ethic (can prioritize, persistent, implementer, and course correct well).

He adds that KieranTimberlake has several people who have grown into this profile and are at different points in the trajectory of their careers.

Note

1 https://medium.com/virtual-reality-virtual-people/jaron-lanier-2298a2d02c2a.

Chapter 3

Roles Superusers play

Having looked at the ten Superuser qualities or attributes, and ten Superuser superpowers, it's time to put these skills into action. What are the specific roles Superusers play on teams, in firms, and in the industry? Firm after firm, Superuser roles fall into predictable categories: they are either generalists or specialists, often falling somewhere along a continuum between the two. Design technology specialists either serve as internal consultants, where they are considered overhead, or integrated into project teams, and billable, or some combination of the two. This chapter looks at each in an effort to determine which approach is more prevalent, and which more effective, resulting in increased value for firms. We'll look at Superuser roles as they compare with more traditional titles within AE organizations, and contrast the differences between generalist vs. specialist design technologists, the generalist/specialist hybrid role, and how teams and firms benefit from this grey space; whether Superusers provide the most value when billable (where e.g. computational design should be billed on a project) vs. overhead; when integrated on teams vs. sitting "in the corner;" and, hands-on vs. primarily strategic, providing leadership or a management role. The chapter concludes by looking at the role of the Superuser in practice: a Superuser team case study.

Superusers as generalists

Does the fact that KieranTimberlake is a research-based practice with an interest in creating knowledge influence their decision of whom to hire? "Everyone here is a designer, researcher, and creator of knowledge through continuous learning," says Matthew Krissel, Partner at KieranTimberlake. "We are all as committed to sharing ideas as we are to creating them. Research, asking questions, and restless curiosity are part of our culture." One has to go back into the recent past to explain why it's important for future specialists to start-off as generalists. Krissel says:

It is important to acknowledge the confluence of other changes that coincided in the mid 2000s. Software and hardware are obvious but more important is the cultural change of sharing coupled with new business models and platforms for design. This evolution, with access to cheap memory and speed was an accelerant for a design environment with significantly fewer barriers to computation, networking knowledge, and exploration in architecture firms.

For me, working on both sides of this offered clarity to the incredible opportunity here. It is also important to remember that this speed and access caused many to not learn some key foundational elements about designing parameters, principles and the mindset around these emerging workflows which are critical skills that too often have been lost.

Something for today's design technologists *is* lost by not first learning analog prior to immersion in the digital. Krissel continues:

Learning to build a perspective by hand is incredibly valuable to working in the computer. This is the same in photography and the continued value in experimenting with film. The foundations of composition, how the human eye works, understanding dynamic range are confronted in analog workflows but software and hardware has unintentionally subverted much of this meaning. This often results in a laissez-faire approach where one will just fix it all in post-production. The need to be aware, conscious, and clear on early decisions impacting modeling, simulation, and visualization downstream are heightened when it is labor intensive to change variables. So, it required great intentionality and purpose in the analog-only era. Being in command of the fundamentals and involved in the design of the early parameters are critical skills for computationally driven practices that seek to do meaningful work.

To be clear, Krissel is not advocating for going back to that earlier, analog time. Krissel emphasizes:

But there is no doubt that parts of working manually are a great precursor and learning tool for working digitally. I would rather we enhance our education to evolve and bring those valuable principles and methodologies forward into a digital workflow. The tactility one feels with a fountain pen, or the joy a well-written piece of code brings us is not the goal. A design practice can and should be about much more than process and diagrams. Even more than the creation of space and the organization of mass and volumes, it is about experiences, connectivity, relationships, movement, time, and the social construct of what the built environment can do.

As a firm, KieranTimberlake has taken the position that everyone must have familiarity with the tools that drive the work. "That does change the dynamic and while not everyone may be authoring content, everyone is expected to be reflective on the work, operating three dimensionally, exploring ideas outside of design reviews, and question it," says Krissel. "This improves the capacity of the whole team and is the foundation of a highly functional collective intelligence model." KieranTimberlake doesn't use the title *Design technologist*. "Labels that separate people by skill compartmentalize them, you're in or you're out," says Krissel. "We prefer specialist which suggests a time-based difference. Someone who is expected to go deeper but it does not mean others are not still accountable to be engaged." So, while their design technologists are referred to as specialists, Krissel emphasizes their generalist natures. "We are a firm of polymaths with people interested in lots of things," adds Krissel. "Some go deeper on fewer things and some go wider on many things, but it never creates a territory for one or another."

Scott Crawford, Principal at LMN Architects says:

Superusers are actually this generation's version of the generalist architect. Antoni Gaudi had a unique process of incorporating simulations, study models, and mockups. I believe this range of tools helped enriched his process and give him a grander view of what he saw as possible, leading to his unique projects that so many are in awe of. This generation's Superusers are approaching practice in a similar way. Designers now have the potential to iteratively study a design through parametric modeling while getting feedback about the performance differences through the use of simulations, and

Figure 3.1
Model build-
ing party in
Scott
Crawford's
personal
shop before
completion
of the LMN
shop. (2018)
Credit: LMN
Architects.

develop highly customized design that can then be constructed through the use of digital fabrication. I believe there is a shift to a more generalist perspective when you can see the design space through the different lenses of each of these tools. The design process is no longer about finding the best of three options, but instead studying the behavior of a combination of decisions, and thereby learning about how decisions affect the performance of the entire system. Because of this, young designers have the ability to quickly establish a depth of experience that previous generations would've taken much longer to develop.

Superusers as specialists

Given how quickly design practice is evolving, is *design technologist* an unnecessary label and/or distinction? According to WeWork's Brian Ringley:

Theoretically my position has always been that the design tech-nologists, or whatever it's popular to call them in a given era, is that it's important to have a small crack team of designers who are able to slowly research and implement new processes in a practice.

There are various models for doing that, and one of the things we were always talking about back on the Design Technology team at Woods Bagot was, "Yeah, right now I'm training users in how to use custom Grasshopper and Revit tools, but ideally that's not my career." Ideally that eventually gets absorbed into the culture of the studio or into the culture of the industry and I move on to the next promising thing, so that we're establishing a reinforcing feedback loop of R&D in architecture.

So where do firms draw the distinction between an architect that knows Grasshopper, Rhino and Revit, and a specialist? "While every architect can work in modeling software, the specialist is charged to move across the office and connect knowledge and expertise," says Krissel. He continues:

When they are not taking on a discrete design problem, they are teaching, guiding, and editing the workflows and habits while introducing new and alternative ways to work. The specialist also has time that is insulated from project demands so they can go deeper and take good ideas that are often crushed under project pressures and develop them further to everyone's benefit.

NBBJ advertises the specialist's role as a design computation specialty. NBBJ Design Computation Leader Dan Anthony explains:

We identify when we need to be doing a better job and when there's a role that needs to be filled. Now it has become specialized … There is still going to be a lot of project design that's expected, but by labeling it a specialist, that makes it part of the active HR exploration. We want to make sure candidates have the skills, having done work that has demonstrated their visual programming skills, some algorithmic design, maybe an interest in fabrication. We look for that in their work.

As discussed in Chapter 1, a distinguishing characteristic of specialists is how devoted they are to coding. According to Anthony:

There are just human differences. There are certain individuals who want to go all the way in, and understand every nuance of the code. Their passion is in the expression of it. They have very little interest in the other parts of it. They don't want to do spreadsheets, or even talk to other people. They really want to dig deep into what they are doing. To bring this topic all the way around, now I work in a workplace practice that designs workplaces, including workplaces for these people. You see very clearly the human needs that they have. They just want darkness, privacy, and a space that does not disturb them.

CannonDesign CTO Hilda Espinal offers a word of caution:

Be careful to do everything in your power not to be pigeonholed as a person that only does "techie things," because I've been there too. It was important to me to advance my career, equally, in both areas and ensure I balanced the two. This is all going to depend on the culture of the office or firm you're at, and their leadership. While you may get to focus on this inter-section in some cases, situations, revolving around life/work balance, may make this experience problematic and having to choose one vs. the other. Unfortunately, you may be pressed by management, particularly middle management to answer "well, pick one role. Which one are you going to do? Because you can't do both. I need you to make my project a priority. I need you to be 100% billable" and so on. Not everyone has caught up with the vision of how crucial these hybrid roles are. As an industry, we still have work to do.

Generalist/specialist hybrid role
Today's practice calls for a range of hybrid roles that fall some-where along a continuum from generalist to specialist. In 2016

Lecture

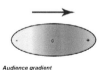

Figure 3.2
Audience
gradient.
(2018) Credit:
DLR Group.

⊕ **Eyes on Hands on**
More than just a passing interest. Want to get in and explore the tools on their own

⊙ **Eyes on Hands off**
Want to see what the tools can do, who can use them but doesn't feel they are able to do the complex inner workings.

⊖ **Reluctant Observer**
Typically skeptical of new tools. Have only a passing interest to confirm to themselves that these "new toys" are fads.

Audience gradient
Over time you are hoping to turn non-believers into creators and users of the best tools.

DLR Group began an effort to inform its design teams and help bring parametric design methodology and computational design tools into their practice. For some, buy-in comes instantly. Why is that? What are some of the mindsets, skillsets, and attitudes of people for whom buy-in is instant vs. may take more time to onboard? DLR Group's Ryan Cameron explains:

> What I have is a series of different users. I ended up discovering something I didn't know existed. I just thought users would be in – or they wouldn't. But that was not the case at all. I have people I call: *eyes-on, hands-off.* I have *eyes-on, hands-on.* And I have *minds-on, everything else is off.* There are some people who want to know about it but don't necessarily want to see it, or touch it themselves. I have people who just want to know that there are certain people in the company who can use it. Then there are people who not only want to see it or watch it but also want to perform the same actions that I am doing.

As explained earlier, KieranTimberlake has people who are vertical thinkers and go deep, and they also have a lot of generalists who move laterally across projects. Krissel elaborates:

> While polymaths touch a lot of things and see possibilities, they sometimes don't go beyond the surface. Deep thinkers expose new layers of an idea but may miss adjacent possibilities. We design our teams with a mix of attributes, experiences, skills, and perspectives and expect that people are open minded, recognize their blind spots and like working in a complimentary way.

This leads to the concept of the Superuser team.

Computational Design Group Leader at Thornton Tomasetti, Hiram Rodriguez, is a polymath who works with all groups at TT, ranging from concept design to construction documents, from rationalizing a building to creating a workflow for a new tool. Rodriguez says:

> For the most part, I am part of the team early on the design stage of the building helping with the rationalization and creating a

61

cohesive workflow. I am also part of monthly talks within different practices. It is key to understand what the current process is in order to create the best workflow. In addition, outreach is a key aspect of my job. We need to make sure we can reach all staff and not only a particular sector. TT is a global office and we have to make sure we are reaching everyone.

In addition to his design talent, LMN Architect's Scott Crawford is an example of a designer who has a considerable number of tools in his arsenal. Does he believe every team and every architect should have these skills? "Absolutely!" says Crawford. He continues:

To me it's an extension of the architect as generalist. I grew up during a time that technology was becoming very accessible with a lot of online resources and I greatly benefitted from exposure to these new tools. That's not to say though that I didn't also get exposed to more traditional tools as well. I learned to draft and construct perspectives when I was in middle school. While I may no longer use some of those skills from my past, they've still contributed to my understanding of how and why things work the way they do. An essential skill within design is the ability to see things from a diversity of perspectives. Experience is one contributor to that diversity and a faculty with a variety of tools is another. Historically, our digital tools were fairly constraining in their functionality, but tools are now getting to the point where there is more opportunity for customization which allows for a designer to essentially design new ways of developing design solutions.

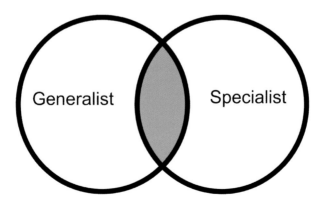

Figure 3.3
A lot of firms benefit from the grey space. (2018) Credit: Deutsch Insights.

Benefitting from the grey space

Shane Burger admits that many people are concerned about their career path and professional development:

> Some of them sit in this position where they can't decide, do I still want to be a project architect eventually? Or do I want to be a specialist? So they sit a little bit in that in-between zone. I had that exact issue in the process of my leaving Grimshaw's office. I was basically put in a position where neither one were being presented to me as a viable option. But Grimshaw benefitted from me sitting in the grey space in between. But in terms of my professional development, I didn't want that anymore.
>
> A lot of firms benefit from that grey space. They can sit and do basic project drawings, but I can also shove them onto a complicated façade and do some SOAR analysis on it. Because there has been no real conversation around that within the prac-tice, it leads it into an unknown space. Then that person is like, I don't know if this is the right place where I want to be. So maybe – I'm in my mid-twenties – I'm going to hop on over to this other firm that's going to give me this specialist's role. And I'll keep hopping around. They either can't decide which of the two they want to be, or they're going to practices that can't decide which of the two they're going to be. The easiest of those paths is to go the project architect route because that's a known career path. Everybody knows what steps you're supposed to go through to eventually become a project architect. Maybe you get named a senior associ-ate. Maybe you become a principal at some point. However, if you're on the specialist side of it, that's really difficult. Because in a lot of practices, including ours, we don't have a clear answer for what you do with specialists in terms of career opportunities and promotion. Can a specialist become a principal has been a huge question? I get asked that sort of thing all the time from my peers when I go to conferences because I'm a principal now. How did you get to be a principal? How does that even work? I have to explain to them, here's the problem. If you want to be a specialist, you then have to decide do you want to remain a subject matter specialist, or do you want to become a manager of specialists? If you go the manager route, that's also a more well-known route. Still more difficult, because a manager of specialists is not as

known a career path within an architecture firm as perhaps in other professions. But if you want to stay a specialist, and you really know your topic, and you want to keep doing that by becoming more and more advanced with it, can you ever become a principal like that? I've not seen a firm that is capable of doing that yet, for someone who doesn't go in to a direction of management.

A collection of specialists does not a team make

We're told in school that once in practice our autonomy won't be valued. We're told to get used to working in teams – because projects have gotten too complex and problems too intractable to work on one's own. Then, once we're in the workforce, we discover that we are indeed valued for our ability to work independently: that there's a time for collaboration, and there are times when we're asked to *just get it done*. Collaboration vs. DIY. Which is it? Team leaders want *both*.

As already discussed, Superusers have the qualities that enable them to work on projects that are team-based and team-focused as well as having the ability, when required, to go deep. There has to be some overlaps between the different roles, explains Burger:

> [b]ecause that enables a better conversation. If you have a collection of specialists who were so specialized that they can't engage with each other, that's not a team at all. I have run into this in the past. Years ago I had a collection of specialists, not actually a team. I spent a long time changing how that works. What has worked best to ensure that they are operating like a team is to be focusing on the end outcomes. Not so much on the technology and the steps that will get us there.

Superuser team case study

Shane Burger provides an example of how Superusers can operate as a team, on a Woods Bagot project in their Jira project environment called Project Collaboration, that asks: *What is the next generation of what we do for design reviews?*

> We started to use this in Jira, epics to describe what are the main things we are doing. Project Collaboration hits a whole lot

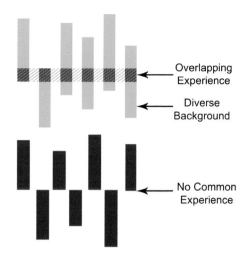

Figure 3.4
Team of
Superusers
(top) vs.
Team of Spe-
cialists
(bottom).
(2018) Credit:
Deutsch
Insights.

Overlapping
Experience

Diverse
Background

No Common
Experience

of things, both internal and external collaboration and communication systems. e.g. our study of Slack within the process is
part of that. One of our epics refers to a desire to better engage
with model-based design reviews. I basically say this is what we're
going to focus on for the next two months. Say, four of us will focus
on model-based design reviews, and the other two of you will work
on something else. That right there, yes it's telling you that we're
already talking about software, or talking about models, but we're
not necessarily saying what software platform we're talking about.
We're not saying which part of the phase we're thinking of,
whether conceptual design all the way through construction documents. We haven't actually answered the question of internal vs.
external. What this is going to mean is I can bring in a group of
people that have a diverse array of skills. I can bring in someone
who is quite strong in terms of Revit and can have a conversation
about what kind of information needs to be in our Revit model to
make its way into a tool. They may have experience with BIM 360
Glue. They may have experience with Revizto – a collection of
different things. I have another person who comes in and has a lot
of experience in tools like Aconex construction management software, but also knows a lot about contractual arrangements associated with collaboration and the protocols for larger-scaled
projects. So he's going to be talking mostly process. Then I have
another person coming in who had been doing some work with me

in the past in VR and is very interested in the kind of interpersonal conversations that happen amongst designers in an augmented environment. How does it work socially?

Then I come in as the person who has been leading this design communication platform development tool where we're building in a design review functionality to it. I'm interested, from a leadership perspective, about how we report upstream the outcomes of reviews. We're all coming from slightly different directions based on our experience and our interests. But we're all trying to meet in the middle to solve the problem that is the same kind of space. It ends up meaning we have a wider conversation around the same thing but from each of our own perspectives. Through that we end up learning the other's perspectives.

For me it's important that I am trying to take advantage of the diversity of backgrounds, skills and interests that might surround a particular thought-space. In this case, around design reviews: What is the next generation of what we do for design reviews?

The role of the Superuser in practice

What proportion should the Superuser be billable vs. overhead?[1] Hands-on vs. strategic? Integrated on project teams vs. providing internal consulting? Going wide vs. deep?

Architect and designer Cory Brugger has a Master's in Engineering from the Product-Architecture Lab at Stevens Institute of Technology, USA. Brugger left Morphosis in 2017 joining HKS as their new CTO. At Morphosis, how much of what Brugger achieved from a design technologist standpoint was project-based? He explains:

The majority of my work came out of projects, but it was always tied to a long-term vision of where the firm was heading. Every initiative and all our R&D was purposeful and viewed as a strategic investment in the future vision of the company. At HKS we've got a variety of internal initiatives and external collaborations aimed at supporting the long-term health of the business. What Heath set up with LINE is very project based. There are two ways that they work. They either help and support other projects throughout the offices, which would be more of a consulting role. They might send one or two people to push through ideas on a design or to implement a new strategy for a project's delivery. Alternatively, they work as a standalone studio and take a project from concept through delivery. We also have a few research groups who are focused on true R&D. They are almost entirely separate from projects which allows them to focus on expanding our industry and market sector expertise.

It is inevitable that one's role evolves and changes as you grow in your career and your value broadens in relationship to a firm's needs. Most recently my role on projects was limited to strategic planning, project set out and review/auditing our models and documentation. Most of my time was sitting in meetings, making sure our teams and project consultants were aligned to a project's goals. Meeting with our clients, contractors, or sub-contractors to go over model uses, and to help support design and delivery processes. Not very much hands-on implementation. That is one of the things I worked on in moving to HKS. We've agreed that 50% of my time should be focused on project or initiative work. We recognize that the actual amount of time will vary depending on the work and initiatives that we have prioritized, but it is still a goal for me to remain integrated into our innovation work.

Typically, the higher one rises within an organization, or in the profession, the less hands-on one is, and the more strategic their focus becomes. As Brugger rose within his previous organization, did he miss the hands-on work? "Yes. I'm not ready to let go," he admits. "Leadership at HKS knew this and it was part of our conversation." Brugger relates it back to medicine:

You want someone who is involved in day-to-day practice to be administering your care. It is important to have somebody who understands the most current tools, processes, and thinking available in practice today – not what was relevant ten years ago. Staying hands-on is important to understand how one's decisions will impact practice and a project's outcome. And by hands-on, I am referring to everything from drafting details to writing code. For example, I've probably written a hundred lines of code in the past six months vs. writing that amount every day. I haven't been doing a lot of platform or plug-in development since I took on a leadership role at Morphosis, so the focus was more on pseudo-code and specifying *what we need the tools to do*. I still think that this is where I will be in my new role, I don't need to write code every day. It's really hard for me. That's not my expertise. I haven't wrapped my head around it often enough to be fluent. There are a lot of people coming up who can do it better than me.

Billable vs. overhead

Each of the Superusers I spoke with for this book works at slightly different percentages when it comes to billable time. "For me, the best balance that we achieve was typically when I had a member of the computation team running about 50/50," says Shane Burger. "So, 50% of their time on direct project work that was billable. And 50% of their time on non-project work development." Burger explains the idea behind this break-down:

> You work on projects, with really difficult problems or amazing opportunities and challenges. Learn from something that was developed there. Then potentially, if you've seen two or three projects run into something similar, use your other 50% of your time to back-up and further develop a more generalized methodology, and potentially a tool. As part of that then, you then go into the next project already having a framework for a tool put together. Or you teach others how to use this tool. You end up having an opportunity where, yes, I'm focusing on one problem on one project, to start thinking multi-project, to then start thinking across the whole enterprise. To then think about how

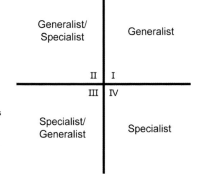

Figure 3.5
Career-wise, your goal is to spend as much time as possible in Quadrant II. (2018) Credit: Deutsch Insights.

can I start to apply this to a larger set of problems? Are there some generalizations that can be brought about from this to think beyond the context of my individual project?

As a Design Computation Leader, NBBJ's Dan Anthony's proportions of work that is strategic vs. hands-on is smaller:

About 25% of my time at this point is strategic. The key to that is not only is that time spent envisioning, but a big part of being a computational specialist is imagining and planning – we're managers – but also have the ability to execute. For instance, we're not going to tell someone what the new process is, we're going to start to build it, and prototype it, writing out portions of our workflow or toolsets that are missing to get that to work properly.

With such a large portion of a leader's time spent on hands-on activities, is there a danger of getting lost in the weeds? Anthony admits:

We always get lost in the weeds. Almost certainly. Maybe it's the joy of the job that there is an opportunity to do that. If I was 100% strategic, it would seem like I wasn't helping to accomplish anything. Occasionally, it feels really good to dive in to a problem, especially a design problem, and provide solutions at a rapid pace.

Anthony finds himself embedded these days in project work. "Which can sometimes be less technical, but it's also where you can sometimes discover new opportunities to apply technology for technique," he explains.

When design technology specialist Jordan Billingsley works on a project specific problem, his time is billable to that project, whereas tool, workflow, and firm-wide office resource development is considered overhead. He says:

I have seen arguments, not at our firm, where they have suggested that a computational designer should be billed on a project, so if a client requests a façade, the most common example, that has some sort of computational design element, that we bill them for computational design work. If anybody's going to become project billable, it'll be the computational designer role.

KieranTimberlake doesn't have "managing partners." That work is distributed across their seven partners to ensure they all still spend most of their time in design. "As a partner, my design agency extends to buildings and the built environment as well as platforms for thinking and making. I create knowledge networks, and help design new workflows, software, and hardware," explains Matthew Krissel. This means he typically runs a 70/30 split with his time:

Roughly 15% of my time is towards Digital Design guidance, editing, testing tools, and mentoring and another 15% of my time is in managing the practice, business development, lecturing. The remainder is spent on multiple design projects and I dial this up and down based on a variety of situations and demands.

While we have an idealized mix or framework it is essential to understand it is highly influenced by situational opportunities and demands so it is critical that what you design can be adjusted on the fly. All specialists at KT must be involved with design work directly on a range of projects. Also, it is important to cut across all projects to ensure they have their finger on the pulse and totality of what's happening here to ensure the stewarding of resources and building skills for immediate needs as well as looking out to future opportunities. They must balance proactive work, the firm goals and digital design strategies while helping to elevate everyone's digital IQ.

Krissel's 60/40 split is made up of 60% on projects, embedded in teams; 20% on office-wide resources, training, knowledge sharing; 20% strategy, building discourse, proactive exploration. For Krissel, the choice between being a specialist and generalist is simple:

Be a specialist and be pervasive throughout the practice. Cultivate a restless curiosity and don't disappear in a corner with your headphones on. Establish your agency and constantly demonstrate your value across typologies and scales, traverse the expected and the unexpected areas of design and engage the strategic and detail parts of the work.

If you compartmentalize yourself, you undermine the most fundamental opportunities of technology and people to expand our design potential in everything we do. Get a seat at the table and help guide architecture in areas beyond just modeling practices, process, and workflows. Proactively engage in the design of new business models, project delivery opportunities, contractual relationships, and the very products we make.

Note

1 See Robert Yori's Design Technology: Billable or Overhead? Two Perspectives, *DesignIntelligence*, October 19, 2015. www.di.net/articles/design-technology-billable-or-overhead-two-perspectives/.

Part two
Finding and making Superusers

Chapter 4

Superusers' value proposition

Superusers see what they do in terms of providing value to others. By engaging Superusers, productivity is increased and value added, via agile processes and automating repetitive processes. This chapter looks at how Superusers provide an improved user experience, by easing use and accessibility of tools, while connecting tools, people, and processes, with an aim to reduce user pain points. The chapter concludes looking at how Superusers seek out and leverage new technologies, and participate in software development, tool creation, and the potential commercialization of these tools.

There are incredible career opportunities brought about by leveraging the new tools. LMN Architects Principal Stephen Van Dyck remembers pulling George Shaw, a partner at LMN, aside in 2010, right before they started the Design/Build phase of their Cleveland project. Van Dyck recalls:

> I had an idea that we could link Grasshopper to Revit to achieve our design intent. We had a really fast delivery timeline and in order to execute our concept, the design and documentation needed to essentially progress in parallel. We knew that there was an API that had just been expanded in Revit, and that with a little bit of coding, we could make these two powerful tools come together. I sure has hell couldn't do the coding myself, but I had faith that one of our founding Tech Studio members, Dan Belcher, could figure it out.
>
> Dan got his head into it and wrote a plug-in we called Cricket. And it worked well for that project, and enabled us to do some pretty amazing things in a really tight schedule and budget. The first product of that tool was the façade for the Cleveland Center for Global Health Innovation, which we built all-up for $65 per

square foot inside to out. I, and the whole delivery team, would credit our design and collaboration process – enabled by that plug-in – to be a key driver in the value we achieved. That plug-in later evolved to become Lyrebird, which Tim Logan, who used to be at LMN, and now with HKS LINE, developed.

As Van Dyck makes clear, the genesis of it all was his conversation with George, and convincing the leadership of the office to explore Revit after years of committing to Bentley. "That was one of those moments where I just knew barely enough on the technical side, and could leverage relationships to suggest a strategic shift, and then get the right people at the table to help make it happen," says Van Dyck.

The value Superusers provide to their teams and firm is not as clear-cut as just delivering code or connecting tools. So what do we mean by delivering value? How is that measured, and what value specifically do Superusers deliver to their teams and firms that employ them? Project Architect at DLR Group Ryan Cameron is interested in providing value to architecture – value created with better design through increased colla-boration, new techniques, and time for reflection. To re-quote Cameron:

Future designers will need all three if they strive to create a better world. They're all dependent on one another. There's an order of operation that almost *has* to happen with these. It's the dewy kind of collaboration that happens between everybody. What are the best techniques you've used to fish-out those best design ideas? You need to do this as quickly as you can to give your brain a chance to catch up with the speed that's out there now. That's the part that is the time for reflection. You really need all three. It's stepping back and describing the pro-cess as simply as possible. It's a bunch of people in a room, scrambling, mad, doing all kinds of sketches, or modeling, what-ever the process is. It's enhanced by technology.

Increased productivity and value via agile processes

People hired from other industries can have an influence, perhaps even improve upon, firm processes and culture. They bring to the AEC industry mindsets and methodologies that help Superusers – and the firms themselves – succeed. Lean, Agile and Scrum are a few that have been introduced into firms in recent years. Woods Bagot principal Shane Burger says:

> Just two weeks ago when I was in our Sydney office, I presented to our design leadership and our CEO. One of the conversations I brought up as part of that was not just lean but thinking about lean management from a global business perspective. But specifically talking about Agile. I walked them through what sort of things does a Scrum-based approach with an Agile provide a project team that is beyond a concern about a project management system? But something that actually yields benefit to the designers. This is a conversation that came up a while ago. My team has been using Jira for its team management for a while but not in a full Scrum format. More of a Kanban style. Rather than specific sprints. But by bringing in people with software development backgrounds it has brought this conversation up.

Burger has two software developers, one in Sydney and one in Melbourne, who are continuing to develop a design dialogue – or design sharing – system within the office. Burger explains:

> It's almost like a Pinterest for projects. We developed that based on a Scrum approach with regular sprints every two weeks now for almost two years. I've been quite used to it now. We're running Jira in that space. We run our team meetings the regular way. We don't have the daily standups because doing that across three geographic locations would have been a bit difficult. That said, we did start to bring on some of those approaches within the core design technology team about nine months ago. We are using it in some way within our team. Now it's moving into a second-level conversation asking, *what can we learn from their approach to potentially apply this to projects?* I'm at the very beginning stages of that conversation. I'm trying to walk people through a narrative of *what does it mean to do this?* What are the regular events that happen along the course of a week or every other week tied to the sprint schedule, and what sorts of benefits do they potentially provide a project team?

This is something that has been changing at Woods Bagot. "Moving out this mentality that there is a single workflow – or single collection of tools – or a single approach that will solve most of the problems that you will run into. For me, it's a lot about agility," says Burger. He continues:

> Both in terms of the toolset you use but also very much the methodology. And having a conversation at the very beginning that says, OK, we need to get from point A to point B, we think we know what point B looks like, but we're not really sure. We at least know that we need to fulfill our contractual obligations. There are 10,000 paths in between so let's discuss where we go first, and make sure we're able, in an agile way, to flow from one place to another. If we need to wire up something new that we've not done before, let's jump into that and learn it. Or bring in the people we need at that moment. It's not a clean process. It's always a messy process. A certain amount of embracing of that is quite important. Understanding at any point we can augment our design process the way that we want to. We can customize what we want to experience and design. It need not be what the software developers – Autodesk or McNeel or anybody – have handed us, and it need not be the way that you've done it for 20 or 30 years that you brought over from SOM or NBBJ or anybody. By its nature, it needs to be as collaborative as possible. The process needs to be developed by the team, customized for whatever the project needs.

Superusers create value in at least four ways: they automate processes; they make tools easier to use, more accessible, reducing pain

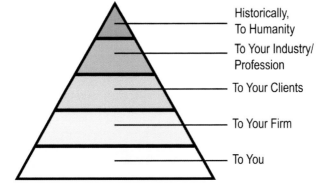

Figure 4.1
Relevance
Pyramid:
Relevant to
whom?
(2018) Credit:
Deutsch
Insights.

Historically,
To Humanity

To Your Industry/
Profession

To Your Clients

To Your Firm

To You

points, providing a better user experience; they connect tools, people, and processes via interoperability; and they seek out new technologies, increasing productivity via software development and tool creation. Let's look at each in order.

Automating processes

Automation is not new. For the design professions, it goes back at least to the advent of CAD. Fernando Araujo, Associate Principal, Studio Leader, and Technical Director of Solomon Cordwell Buenz (SCB) was hand drafting and then at some point picked up CAD. At the time, there was CAD, and there was CAD the way Fernando Araujo did it. This was the early- to mid-1990s and he would hit the macros on the keyboard with his left hand, and the whole building seemingly instantly materialized.

Superusers isn't about people who literally use software better or faster than others. One can find outliers at industry events winning contests for doing that. Instead of getting people to work faster, one might purposefully slow people down – to get them to think before they act: that's a Superuser tactic or skill. But back in the day, at the introduction of CAD to the industry, it was literally the ability to use a new tool and make the most of it, and Fernando Araujo was someone who had that ability. Araujo admits:

> That was probably me. Back at that time CAD was fairly new and we had perhaps five or eight workstations. It was a limited amount of workstations so most of the people were still drafting by hand, especially the senior folks. But my being a more junior person at the time, and interested in technology, I came there and knew a lot about CAD. And I did. I was pretty good with the macros as I do recall. I still use them if I use CAD. I use the short macros, I don't use the pull downs, because it's just a lot faster to type in a command, a two letter command and then move as opposed to finding it on pull down. Yeah, I do remember that.

So, in a sense Fernando Araujo was automating with the macros before anyone else was really automating in architecture. He took a relatively nascent tool and made it really sing and perform. What enabled him to do that? Was it his education at the earlier Mies program at IIT, and afterwards working at Mies's successor firm? What would lead one to think – beyond his interest in technology – that by using two fingers on the keyboard in CAD, he'd become the equivalent of a team of one putting a building together? What was behind that? Araujo explains:

Going back to when I was at Fujikawa Johnson, CAD was a new thing. My boss was so skeptical about CAD. He thought it was just the biggest waste of time, yet everybody was investigating it so we'd experiment with it. There were so many senior people and knew so much more than I did, but they weren't interested at all in learning or using CAD. I saw it as an opportunity and it seemed interesting to me. I got sucked into the idea of the technology, even back then, of being able to do the work of multiple people much more quickly. I just jumped in. I thought, I'm going to learn this, and it will help me find my place and be of value to the firm, and help the firm advance. It was a good opportunity for me as a young person with a little bit of knowledge to really experiment and help the firm push a little bit and see where we could go with CAD, which was the big thing back then.

Which takes us to automation today and Superusers automating things. CAD aside, some if not most of what design technologists do today didn't exist in the early 2000s. Hiram Rodriguez, Computational Design Group Leader at Thornton Tomasetti, was not aware of the various visual scripting platforms until he was in school. "It is just insane when we do retrofits of old buildings, and you get to see the construction set, they really crammed all the data in a few sheets," says Rodriguez. He continues:

Whereas today, current technology is furthering our ability to generate complex shapes and forms, that need complex construction sets. It is hard for me to visualize this profession 20 years ago without access to tools like Rhino, Revit and other cloud-based platforms that allow geometry to be "easily" translated to other platforms. Within TT, we encourage the use of new technology. We have found that by using and trying different technologies and techniques, we have a better understanding of the built world. It has allowed us to approach design from different perspectives and deliver a higher standard of data.

For example, Rodriguez only had two days to come up with a few roof iterations for a competition and the only way to coordinate all the iterations was by using Grasshopper. He says:

> The tool allowed us to generate BIM data, steel tonnage and surface roof area for ETFE. This was crucial for us. We end up winning the competition, which allow others to see the power of these new processes within the firm. In the near future, it is going to become even easier to use these tools, but if we don't create tools that are user-friendly, they will never be adopted. We should also focus on teaching how to generate consumable scripts. No one wants to open a massive Grasshopper script. Can we think about creating plug-ins or add-ons instead?

Computational designers look for any part of the work process that's repeatable, assess what repeatable tasks are worth automating, and which should be left as they are. "Sometimes the problem, to automate a task is too much of an effort, it's better to chop it up and break it into segments that you can tackle," explains Rodriguez. "Because it would take half a year's worth of the developer's time to develop a tool. Then is it really worth it? That's always the question." Rodriguez continues:

> You always want to approach visual scripting in terms of tasks or parts that function together, because that is the whole purpose of these platforms, especially in Grasshopper or Dynamo. As you build these complex systems you need to start thinking how the structure functions in real life. You don't want to build secondary systems when your primary systems have not been rationalized. The script should be flexible so that you can break those elements into major elements that are going to control smaller elements and then you start focusing down on those elements and their relationships. This is crucial when building complex form relationships for any project in Grasshopper or Dynamo.

"When people see for the first time how quickly you can emulate a design configuration with minimum input, I hear the phrase, 'You're just going to automate the whole profession out of a job!'" says Ryan Cameron. "That immediately puts 'non-Superusers' into a defensive mode." He asks, "If clicking a few buttons puts you out of a job, should you be doing that job in the first place?"

AI: augmented and informed vs. being fully automated

Woods Bagot is engaged in a project to look through their standard delivery processes to think about how much they can automate. "That's a pretty big conversation," says Shane Burger. "We're basically going step by step, saying Project A needs to put together a PDF set and upload it into this system and end up with these people." Burger continues:

> We're trying to go through this process where we simplify and further develop a lot of our delivery management processes that we use in the practice. What we started discussing was UK delivery standards vs. other regions, to take what I would argue was a 1980s or 1990s method of management and update the whole system. The second step of that is to start looking through those gaps in process. Those things that are very repeatable tasks that we do all the time, and start to look for easier ways to automate them.

Figure 4.2
Social virtual reality at CannonDesign TiP. (2018) Credit: Laura Peters.

But what specifically is meant by *automating processes*? One example that's on the more opportunistic side is where Woods Bagot, which has a very large interiors practice, is starting to think about stronger connection points between their Revit libraries and how they manage their libraries of content, the method with which they develop their cut sheets and track their use of products across the company, and right now, what is a manual generation in Microsoft Word or InDesign of that delivery package to the client. Burger explains:

> These are things that we do again and again and again. And we might as well automate that. We did another one that is a basic urban site study step. It was 20 pages of content that would typically take somebody 2–3 days to do in Illustrator and AutoCAD. We basically automated that process and turned it into a 20-minute step. Andrew Heumann worked with me on that one. We spent 4–5 days and built this thing up to automate something that we do at the beginning of every single project in New York City. It just comes up all the time, so we always produce this content. I wouldn't call this AI so much. It's just pure mechanization. We're just trying to automate a lot of these steps that are in there.
>
> I don't have a firm position on where we, as individual humans and designers, are going to provide a greater level of expertise than what we can get out of an AI. I am of the opinion that we underestimate what the AI will be capable of doing in the long term. This goes back to Amara's Law [*We tend to overestimate the effect of a technology in the short run and underestimate the effect in the long run*]. Everybody's going to be talking about AI designing stuff for us in five to ten years. No, but there's a pretty good shot that it will hit it in 20 years or more. And more so than we think it is going to. We're going to be pretty surprised at the kind of stuff that's going to be there. It's simply going to be a question of where we think human judgment is going to provide a unique value over somewhere else. We shouldn't be the people doing code reviews or any of that stuff that is documented as a process in a manual somewhere and you simply have to go through the steps to do it. You should effectively then have an augmented interface that's provided to you that gives you warnings, notifications, or a solution space to work within that always satisfies the conditions that are necessary. But then you have to take the judgment that says, OK,

when it deals with prioritization of those factors in the solution space, I am going to play around with it and say this is more important or this is more important. Safety and such will always trump everything else. But at least it puts you in a position where all those automated checks that we typically have to go through on projects, there's no reason any of us should be doing this stuff. I would be perfectly happy for that stuff to go away.

Burger describes an augmented and informed approach to design that is not automated:

What I am starting to think about is a ubiquitous heads-up display for design. That might even be something like – we've talked about it with our workplace sectors at Woods Bagot, whether interiors, lifestyle, or residential – a display that might be specific to the typology or sector that you're going after that provides you with information to keep you up to date as you're working through the design.

That was even part of the approach with the user interface work that I was doing with Brian Ringley and Andrew Heumann. It's not always something that you want to input into, but that you want to receive feedback on while you're working through the process. This augmented and informed approach is going to be increasingly important for any of those things that are not going to be fully automated.

Do we need to fear that by automating what we do, design professionals will eventually lose their jobs? Repeatable automatable tasks that are broken down into their constituent parts are referred to as *deskilling*. The word implies, especially with machine learning, that the algorithms will pretty much do what we're currently doing, and in the long run, in perhaps 20 or 30 years, it'll put us out of at least that job. "In the AEC industry, it is a bit harder for automation to completely take the role of an architect or the engineer," says Hiram Rodriguez. He continues:

However, we may have tasks within these roles that will benefit from a complete automation, allowing us to focus on other things. The AEC industry has too many problems to solve right now. One of them is the data is not the same in some of the industries, so we need to come up with ways to create standards that will help all industries moving forward.

User experience

Ease of use, accessibility, reduction of pain points – these are all examples of an improved user experience, value-added that's the result of working with a Superuser. According to Rodriguez:

> In terms of accessibility, some people don't realize this, but visual programming tools, like Grasshopper and Dynamo, were invented because we're more visual in the design field or architecture and structures that we need to visualize something ... But then even then, some people just look at that and see it as spaghetti. Then you come up with plug-ins like Human UI that make visual programming tools easier to use.

Do design technologists see making tools useful for everyone as a form of user interface (UI/UX)? Do computational designers need to have the ability to lift the hood on tools right out of the box to customize them to make them user-friendly? "Yes and yes," says NBBJ Design Computation Leader, Dan Anthony:

> The idea is that we do complex things for a clear reason. We're increasingly calculating more difficult problems and solving more complicated design challenges. But we're doing it for some kind of clear goals. Especially when you think about something like machine learning coming into the field in the form of design augmentation, it's only going to be useful if a designer or someone in another role who is working on a project is able to understand the intent or purpose, how to apply it, and how to cycle through it. It's all about user experience. In the near term, it's hard to see how we're going to put things in human's hands that are going to be easy to work with. Things like the voice-activated tools (e.g. Google's home tools or Amazon Echo's Alexa, that are able to easily transmit complicated knowledge to people) with really nice mobile design, hint at intuitive processes but also can communicate complex ideas ...
>
> But at the same time, one of the best things that has been happening, and one of the things we should strive for, is that when you find that the basic problem isn't solved by that clear interface [here we go back to the title of the book] your regular user is going to need a slick interface that helps them understand things. The

85

Superuser is the person who knows that you can lift the hood. And that when you do lift the hood, say to an Autodesk product, that there is a clear API, that's still easy to navigate, and lets you connect/reconnect items. That's why visual programming has been so successful. It has made Superuser status a little more attainable. These are very complementary positions to be in. Because there are times when I don't want to be writing the API interfaces. I want to at a certain point land at a tool that's going to be useful.

Google Cardboard, to use IrisVR's Ana Garcia Puyol's phrase, is a down and dirty, cheap technology. It's ten bucks! What role does an entry level tool like that play in inspiring experimentation and messing with tools? Garcia Puyol admits:

If you had given me a $30,000 piece of equipment, I wouldn't have dared to dream. I would have thought, "yeah, this is so cool, this is the future, but not the present." For me, that particular evening, I thought, "This is it, this is what I'm going to make my immediate future about." It was what I could get to work on and it was accessible. It's funny because now I don't do any work with the Google Cardboard and it's more something very entry-level, a backdoor tool for many people. I went to TT and created a proof of concept over the weekend relying on affordable technology. That couldn't have happened with a very expensive piece of technology. What would have been the point to build something for users that doesn't exist yet, for users who cannot afford it? Because, even now, we still struggle with it. If VR takes off, it's still expensive. But if VR had been a piece of technology that's very, very expensive, then why would you invest in that? It makes me think of Tesla and SpaceX and how some people just really bet on very expensive technologies with the goal of making them cheaper eventually and that's great. But on my end, I wasn't building hardware. I was building software. For the success of my initial idea and even what we do here: you're building on top of a technology or a piece of hardware that has to be accessible for people. Otherwise, you're doomed.

"My YouTube web series has taught me that this culture isn't for everyone, but that doesn't mean only certain people can use high technology," says Ryan Cameron. He continues:

The key is making it accessible, easy to use and, if you're really good, make it fun. Most people don't need to understand what's under the hood, they just want to learn to drive. I do believe that design professionals need a basic understanding of what data means to them if they are to succeed.

Interoperability: connecting communications, processes, and people

As already mentioned, Brian Ringley and Andrew Heumann worked on Wombat when they worked at Woods Bagot. "That stuff is fun and valuable and it's fun to promote, but you go to RTC or BILT, and AU, and it gets a little tiresome," says Brian Ringley, now with WeWork. He continues:

It might also just be where I'm at. I've gone through various phases of interest and I actually think it was really interesting timing for Flux to drop that product. But I also felt like they had ushered in the era of interoperability.

I am interested with the history of what's going on with just the idea of open data. I do feel like they helped popularize and usher in an era of JSON web plug-ins for exchanging data, and then people are like, "Okay, I can do that, too, or I can make my own sauce." Do I think that is what is actually the biggest crisis facing the architectural business model? No. That's why Flux didn't make enough money. It's hard looking back, because as somebody who was very close with them early on and very excited about the tools, it was

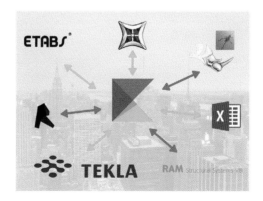

Figure 4.3
Konstru BIM interoperability platform. (2018) Credit: Thornton Tomasetti CORE Studio.

like, "Well, of course I was excited, it made my life so much easier," and it made a meaningful impact on the way we deliver buildings. Bjarke Ingels' The Eleventh project is rising out of the ground right now, and that was absolutely made easier through the use of Flux. Could we have done The Eleventh project without it? Sure. It would have been a lot more painful. It's hard because you see the immediate value as somebody who has the expertise, and especially somebody who's working with complex geometry versus more standardized architecture, but ultimately when you see it go, you're not surprised. It's hard to beg a firm to pay that much money for it because that's not the biggest problem facing firms … It was never connecting the tools. It was connecting communications and connecting processes. Maybe it's just because there have always been manifold solutions to it. It wasn't like, "Oh, my God! How do I go back and forth between Rhino and Revit?" It was "How do I work with all of my consultants? How do I manage all of that data to meet deadlines?" That's not tools.

Seeking new technologies: software development and tool creation

The best architects and engineers build their own tools – that's the design profession's new reality. "With the proliferation of Grasshopper and now Dynamo, we now can build almost any tool to do anything we want. The more experience we get with that, the more powerful that will become," says Stephen Van Dyck. "For the most complicated problems, our tool is crafted by us. I believe that when we can design our tools, we get much better outcomes." If not creating their own

Figure 4.4 Announcement for the public release of Wombat, the design computation software authored by Andrew Heumann and Brian Ringley at Woods Bagot. (2018) Credit: Woods Bagot.

tools, do Superusers proactively seek out new technologies – or do so reactively, by waiting for others to bring them to their attention? "There is definitely a proactive element," says Dan Anthony:

> One thing that I personally feel deficient in is that I don't always stay socially active e.g. on Twitter. Part of it is that I sometimes have a hard time getting through the chaff of it – there is a lot of noise in that space. But I do think following *asocial* media is important – I do track it. Research is another very important part of this. And I do a lot of research. It's about leaving space to explore what's available. It's part of my job to do this. It's not time that I have on the books. But something I think is critical to succeed at my job. A lot of times we have these clear goals where we really want to figure out a way for doing something. The risk for us is that we start down a path where we're trying to reinvent the wheel. I grew up with the Internet as a way of solving that problem by searching for that information. Reaching out to people, asking them questions, is a great way to solve that problem. The key is that you do a really thorough job of exploring what the state of affairs is, by digging through GitHub, by reading journals to see if anyone has tried to solve this before. Sometimes they don't want you to know that they've tried to solve this problem.

And when technologies cannot be found, Superusers create them. KieranTimberlake is a firm that not only leverages the latest technology but creates its own tools. As partner Matthew Krissel explains:

> It is important to note that making a digital tool can be a simple script that may only take an hour to make, and people make them on their own all the time. Other tools might require a few days or even years. So, our process calls for an objective assessment of multiple possible outcomes. It is important that we first look for existing tools as we are not interested in making things just because we can. We test multiple tools before we start to invest in making one. When we are testing tools to purchase or that we made you always do it on real projects, with real teams and deadlines in order get the kind of assessment that is useful.
> In all cases, one answers a series of questions, like: What is the need? Do we already own something similar? What will this

allow us to do that we cannot do now? Have you tested it? What is the workflow? What agency will it provide? Is this hardware, standalone software or a plug-in? Is this on premise or cloud hosted? What are the costs? Purchase or subscription? Is this project specific or firm wide applicability? This is then evaluated by a small group of the firm's decision-makers and they determine that if it exists, they may green light the purchase or do an extended demo on a real project. If one does not exist, we do a deeper analysis to determine if we should build it.

This involves setting goals and defining the objectives and what problem it would solve, market research and gap analysis within and outside our industry. If positive, we then build a proof of concept and conduct an assessment and feasibility review, asking: Is it desirable? Anybody want it? Is it feasible? Is it viable? Can it be done? If we proceed, then it's into further design, refinement, build partnerships, gather feedback.

It is also worth noting that the need for tools arises in many ways. Sometimes we identify needs through conversations within our Digital Design platform. We have created five task teams that cut across and touch just about everything in our practice to drive the computational discourse. 1) knowledge acquisition, 2) knowledge management, 3) BIM practices 4) visualization practices, 5) near future practices. Each task team meets weekly or biweekly, building discourse around these areas of practice, so all kinds of needs bubble up. The task team leaders help prioritize, coordinate, and make resources available to address them. Needs are also identified in the Tools and Workflow sessions. And sometimes, a need or idea simply comes up during the flow of design on a project.

Figure 4.5
Superusers
want to be
on top of
emerging
technologies.
(2018) Credit:
Deutsch
Insights.

Commercialization of tools

In recent years it has become popular to say that every firm needs to be a software firm. More critical, perhaps, is the importance of elevating everyone's digital IQ. Krissel says:

> The comfort with and ability to make tools is important, but that does not mean EVERY firm needs to become a software firm. Unfortunately, there are people leading firms who have no idea what tools people are using. No idea why they use one over the other. Every person up and down the firm may not necessarily be using the full kit every day, but there are many ways that everyone's digital IQ should be elevated in the industry ...
>
> Regardless if people are authoring content, modeling geometry, or running a simulation or none of the above, I think it is important that the people in a practice know the what and why, otherwise they will never really be able to get behind the work. Once you elevate everyone's digital IQ, you start making lots of little and large improvements. Not necessarily to always commercialize, but to improve the day to day, and increase opportunities and expectations for the people around you and the projects.

The commercialization of tools does create an opportunity area for firms. "Yes, there is lots of room here for firms large and small as there is no shortage in sight for improving how we work together and understand the work," says Krissel. He continues:

> Commercializing software is not easy and becoming too obsessed with it in an architecture practice can create some unfortunate motivations that can detract from one's capacity to do great projects. You must go back to those first principles of why you are practicing architecture. If it's about making tools only, then perhaps you should become a software company. If it's about making great architecture, and you happen to make tools when the project demands it, you're an architect who can make tools. Designers making software and hardware as well as designing buildings should not be mutually exclusive endeavors, rather they reflect our time in history and our path forward. These business sectors will continue to blur. The real question is, what are you in this for? Answer this and the rest takes care of itself.

Chapter 5

Hiring (and poaching) Superusers

Over the years I've helped firms with searches to fill design technologist and design technology leader roles. My own experience doing
searches, looking for design technologists, and design technology
leaders with both hands-on and strategic skills – while they do exist,
they are also very hard to find. A few years back I was asked to
assist with a search for a well-known architectural design firm for a
design technologist. It was after the 2008 downturn in the economy,
and throughout the industry employees were expected to do the
work of two, or even three – their own work, and that of those who
were let go or had left on their own. When workloads increased,
instead of hiring, employees were expected to absorb the additional
work. Fees hadn't recovered to their pre-2008 level, so firms in many
cases had no other choice. So when it came to find a design
technologist, this firm essentially initiated a search for two people:
someone who was hands-on, could be integrated on a team, and be
billable – and someone who was more strategic and forward-thinking,
whose time would be considered overhead: only they wanted these
abilities in the same person. A worldwide search was undertaken, and
while a few promising candidates were identified, no one could quite
fill their expectations.

Just a few years later, it's a different story. Today, design
technologists – and especially design technology leaders – are
expected to be both hands-on and to have a strategic outlook from
which the firm can benefit. Filling this role, while never a slam-
dunk, has become easier. Some of my own architecture major
students who minor in computer science, after a few years out in
the field, would be ideal candidates for such a role. Following the
advice and suggestions in this chapter should make the process
easier still.

Searching for design technologists

Some firms, especially those who have seen how hard it can be to hire from outside their firm, opt to grow them from within. The key is to keep constantly on the lookout, not just when you're in need of filling a position, and not to let finding a promising candidate with lesser technology skills dissuade you from having a conversation. This chapter looks at the seemingly never-ending search to find design technologists – identifying, recruiting (and the reality of poaching) Superusers, leadership and design technologist buy-in, and hiring Superusers as a design challenge, concluding with hiring for tool virtuosity vs. soft skills, interpersonal intelligence, and social awareness.

Where does one find design technologists – professionally and geographically? We'll look at hiring design technologists externally, internally, and from other industries and educational backgrounds, and consider the pros and cons of employing and engaging them. Design technologists come from within architecture, architectural education, or branch off from architecture firms to become in-house design technologists or design technology consultants. Strategists vs. doers: this is the recruitment challenge. In this chapter, design technologists share their insights and experiences on how they find good people to fill design technologist roles.

How you hire anyone is how you hire everyone

When Morphosis hires, they appear to do so behind strong recommendations. What is behind those recommendations? "A portfolio and interview are always a large part of any hiring process; however, the one thing Morphosis does well is using their internship program as an alternative to direct hiring," explains Cory Brugger, Director of Technology at Morphosis from 2010–2017, now CTO of HKS. He continues:

> That is one of their biggest avenues as far as bringing on new staff. A large portion of the staff in the office started as an intern, and they either get it or they don't. They have three month, six month and one-year evaluations. At any given time they can have six to ten interns in the offices. At best one or two a year become full-time employees. This is great for entry level and junior staff, but you're always balancing your resources within an office.

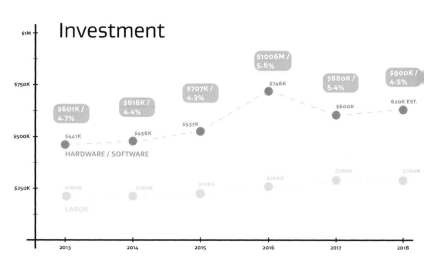

Figure 5.1
CO Architects' technology investment over five-year span for both labor and hardware/software, averaging around 4.8% of net revenue. (2018) Credit: CO Architects.

Morphosis conducted an audit every year to see where they were in terms of staff resources and technology. Brugger continues:

This is where we are improving, this is where we have weaknesses, this is how either resources, process and/or technology can help that. It was always a way for us to have a conversation about how to move forward. At one point we started to notice that we had this huge gap in mid-level architects. We had these big projects coming up at the time that were starting to get into DD and CDs and, there was a noticeable talent gap. We needed people to be able to help manage drawing sets and understand what we are working towards for deliverables. We were very heavy at the top and very heavy at the bottom. To address this, we're relying on our network within the industry to find the right people. You can teach somebody how to be an architect, and you can teach them new tools, but you have to start with someone who has personal drive, and the ambition to engage in a broader conversation about architecture. It is much more about personality: mindset, attitude, etc. If you want to be part of changing something as stodgy and engrained as the AEC industry, you have got to have a lot of ambition and pretty thick skin. This industry isn't going to change that quickly.

How about specifically concerning the hiring of design technologists? "On the technology side, we were running one or two tech interns per year," says Brugger. "People who were working with us on global tools and doing R&D. We typically hired one full time person per year from this group. Sarah Kott, Viola Ago, and Michelle Lee added a ton of value to the office."

Design technologist and leadership buy-in

Jordan Billingsley's firm, Hord Coplan Macht, starts their search strategically, seeking input from their people committee and their student engagement committee, to decide which traits they need to look for. For Billingsley, the process is much more intuitive:

> For me it's really easy, because whenever you catch eyes with someone and you both know something, you just have this feeling. You both understand what we're talking about. There's that non-verbal shorthand, and when someone's able to describe a very complex problem in very simple terms, or describe a very complex project in great detail, people know that they have not just read some buzzwords on ArchDaily, and put something together in an interview so that they can get a job that should have a little bit higher salary.

One of Billingsley's hiring objectives is to have his firm's leadership recognize the value of visual programming skills to better recruit like-minded people. "Once you get people to be aware of automation and the benefits of it, then they start thinking, 'What else can we automate?'" says Billingsley. "Someone at my firm described this mindset best by translating the thought of, 'I wish we had an intern to do this task' to 'Can we automate this?'"

How often are design technologists themselves involved in the hiring of design technologist staff? Billingsley says:

> My position, historically, has not been involved in the hiring, but it has been more involved lately. I requested it. What it came down to was they recognized that I wasn't able to put more time towards training. So I said, "Look, I don't have any more time for training, so we need to be smarter about who we hire." It's not only those who come out of school without any experience. We still give them a shot. We are looking for mental sharpness and ability to learn and eagerness, all of the same things that our

hiring committees have traditionally looked for still remain. I just add a little bit of a filter for specific traits.

How do firms find good people? And who in the firm is, and who isn't, involved in the hiring process? Dan Anthony says:

> There are two parts to this question: one is organizational, the other is the search and how we identify talent. At NBBJ, we're lucky that Design Computation Leaders actually do have a say and people trust us. We're always on the lookout. We identify when we need to be doing a better job and when there's a role that needs to be filled. Now it has become specialized. We advertise the role as a design computation specialty. There is still going to be a lot of project design that's expected, but by labeling it a specialist, that makes it part of the active HR exploration. We want to make sure candidates have the skills, having done work that has demonstrated their visual programming skills, some algorithmic design, maybe an interest in fabrication. We look for that in their work. The three computational leaders will interview leads, and pass on those leads to studios and say, hey, we think this person has a unique skillset that suits the requirements for this area. We also say, they may be good designers.

As for who decides who gets hired and who doesn't, at NBBJ it's up to the studio to make the final determination about their fit. "We still at this point don't have much authority in whether the person is hired or not," admits Anthony. "But we try to recommend talented individuals. The way we find those individuals varies. In order to find talent, you have to be out there looking for talent. We really try, as much as we can, to do that."

KieranTimberlake has a both/and solution when it comes to deciding who decides whom to hire. "The stakes and the investments in architecture are high, so it is important that firm leaders and younger staff are involved in evaluating resumés as well as interviews and hiring decisions," says Matthew Krissel. "We like to pair an experienced interviewer with a less-experienced one, so you get a multi-generational, multi-perspective take on somebody." In terms of finding specialists, KieranTimberlake has had the best luck promoting from within.

nvestment

Figure 5.2
CO Architects' investment in dedicated technology staff over five-year period evolved from a focus on desktop/IT support to additional dedicated digital technology designers. Digital technology staff is complemented by project-centric staff with digital and computational design skillsets. (2018) Credit: CO Architects.

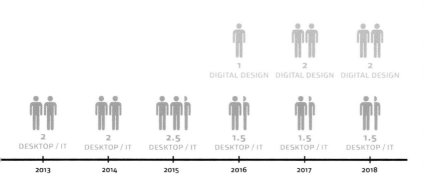

Finding, recruiting (and poaching) Superusers

So, where are design technologists found? "You don't find them straight out of college," says Billingsley. "You either have to develop them internally, or you have to recruit." And when he says "recruit," how does he recruit? "Well, I didn't want to say 'steal' or 'poach' but you basically you have to," says Billingsley. He continues:

I'll be at some happy hour and there'll be the CEO, and they're going around the room talking to the young people, which is weird, and then they come to talk to you and they're, "Where do you work at and what do you do?" And then immediately, they say, "Well, if you ever want to come work for us, here's my card."

We've all seen this behavior. It seems like everybody does it. Today, they don't say "steal," they say "poach." Until recently, nobody used the word "poach," not publicly, and now everyone's admitting to doing it. *Oh, that person you're talking about, are they good? Great. We'll give them a call in the morning, and steal them.*

In Chapter 2, Shane Burger described superpowers for his core team members: being a problem solver; an ability to figure it out; a thirst for learning the next thing; being good at teaching; having good conversational skills, among others. He admits:

What I have basically described to you – there aren't a whole lot of people who have those kinds of skills. Which is why everybody's fighting for them. And everybody's poaching them from everybody else. It becomes important for me to look for some of those things, especially in some of the younger people coming out of the university. I just lucked-out that I ran into a woman I thought who was fantastic in our Sydney studio, when I was there a few weeks ago. Very junior in terms of skills. But already has some of this mindset. Especially around the thirst to learn, to problem solve, and to teach. And even though she kept apologizing, saying *I don't have the same technical skills as some people*, I told her you seem to have the right mind to pick them up. I'm less concerned about that. That's easier to teach.

Hiring powerusers

What about hiring advanced users of the tools? Are there certain things to look for in a candidate, especially someone with the skillsets of a software developer? "We need everybody," says LMN Architects Principal, Stephen Van Dyck. He continues:

> We need the people who understand enough about technology to make it more fundamental to our process. We also need the people who know how to execute technically really well. For us right now, I would say our pinch point is that second group. We've got a lot of staff that understand the basics of Grasshopper and other advanced tools well, but don't use them regularly enough to be powerful users. Grasshopper in particular is one of those platforms with an exponential performance curve: the more you know, the better you are, and it gets increasingly more powerful at a steep rate. You've got to have those experts. But you've got to have the people who can strategize and think about how the tool can be applied.

LMN Architects has found that some people just don't want to do the strategy – some people just like to immerse themselves in solving technology problems. Should firms look for both of those qualities in the same person? "Yeah," says Van Dyck, "But maybe that's a unicorn!"

Hiring as a design challenge

In what ways is hiring a design challenge? "I read in Ed Catmull's book, *Creativity Inc.*, that 'If you give a good idea to a mediocre team, they

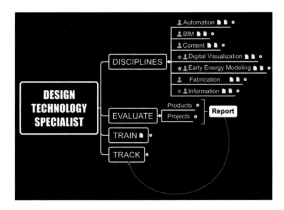

Figure 5.3
Design tech-
nology spe-
cialist mind
map. (2018)
Credit:
Jordan
Billingsley.

will screw it up. If you give a mediocre idea to a brilliant team, they will either fix it or throw it away and come up with something better,'"[1] says Matthew Krissel. He continues:

When we're hiring, we meet for an hour each week to discuss who we met with and where everything stands. Between the resumés, work samples, and the interviews we have a pretty good sense of someone's design skills, how facile they are with tools, and how well-spoken they are.

It is harder to discern how they react under pressure or in a time crunch. How collaborative are they really? Can they synthe-size ideas? Can they read between the lines to really extend a nascent idea? It's one thing to memorize a few questions so you look for how natural question asking comes to them. Do they see inquiry as a design tool? How well do they take a critique? Are they quick to make excuses or blame others? Or when we start to debate something, do they riff on ideas and get excited about building something together? Almost everything we do here is driven by a small group and not just one or two people. It is remarkable what small groups of talented people can do, but part of the design challenge is how we organize ourselves and certainly hiring and mentoring plays a key role.

When people already have a design technology bent, certain firms are the first that they think of, firms that exploit the technology. When you're not on the design technologist's radar, does that make it harder for firms to find good design technology people? "I guess I'm going to find that out soon, because we have some positions that just got posted," says Hilda Espinal, CTO at Cannon-Design. There are two ways Espinal has been able to recruit people to the team:

> Through the connections everyone has, because, let's face it, you don't come out of school with a degree that enables you to be the CTO of an architectural firm. So, networks, I'm still going to leverage that. But also, let us not undermine leading by example, externally and internally. Externally, I've been doing a fair amount of publications and speaking events, which seem to attract talent's interest. Internally, just about everywhere I've been in this position, almost always somebody (architect, interior designer, engineer, you name it!) says, "Hilda, I'm interested in doing what you do." Almost always followed by *how did you get there?* And then that almost always eventually leads to, "I want to give it a try, I have an aptitude for this."

Tool virtuosity vs. soft skills

Hiring is hard. It's hard to predict who will stick and who won't. What are some of the things one should look for when hiring that are predictors for success? What, in other words, are Superuser qualities to look for when hiring? When Matthew Krissel, Partner at Kieran-Timberlake is interviewing someone, he looks for the following ten attributes in candidates:

1. Creative, with a good design sensibility and capable of seeing the big picture and the details. We like people who enjoy working at multiple scales.
2. Curious, observant, resourceful, and listens well. Asks smart questions, can draw out insight and synthesize ideas effectively. We look for ways to understand how observant they are. As a designer, it is critical to be always looking and learning from the world around you. Then, can they project these observations forward into actionable design?
3. Comfortable with uncertainty. An elastic mind and process that is responsive to change, can course correct, and remain motivated. How did you respond and how did you move forward?

4. A penchant for research, data, and objective analysis. Can operate laterally and vertically, and is interested in continuous learning.
5. Critical thinker, is open minded, and knows when to extend an idea and when to pull back.
6. Well organized, excellent at prioritizing, and works well independently and collaboratively.
7. Works intelligently, efficiently, and is tool agnostic. Especially in environments where they have been exposed to a lot of tools. Do they just keep going with the first thing they learned? Or are they constantly trying to learn new things, to see how they work, stretch their abilities? Are they willing to learn something new because it's the right tool for the job even if it is one they are less familiar with?
8. Works fluidly across multivariant design concepts with persistence and optimism.
9. Well spoken. Can speak about the design process, an idea, or the project with clarity. How insightful and reflective are they on their work?
10. High standards, shared values, and interest in our mission, our work, and can help us get to where we want to go.

"Obviously, no one hits every single attribute, especially people right out of school or new to the field, so you want to see their capacity to evolve and acquire these qualities," says Krissel. He continues:

We are deeply connected to the success of everyone at the firm and take seriously our role in each person's professional development. We pair new employees with mentors for regular and informal feedback. We encourage informal reviews and discussion while also having structured performance reviews at three months, six months, and annually with a mix of people involved in each review. We want to give clear and frank assessments and advice to support the growth we expect from everyone and hear their ideas about ways we can improve.

If you have made it to the interview your work has been analyzed and debated. We already know if you can draw, model, and have some graphic design sensibility. Questions around how one works, their command of the tools available to them, how they adjust in the flow of design and the choices they make are a part of the interview. At the same time, I want to draw a distinction. While we are encouraged by tool virtuosity, one cannot be so easily persuaded as it does not always translate to a great designer, or collaborator. Tools can be learned so we look for more of the soft skills, habits, motivations, and a person's mindset. We're happy to train people as we see ourselves as always learning as well. We're happy to give people the tools they've never tried before to elevate the work. But they must be interested in mastering new skills and, of course, have the aptitude and motivation to do it well.

Career path cases: part I

There are as many career paths taken by technology trailblazers in the AE profession and industry as there are technology trailblazers. Here, in their own words, are testaments to what can be achieved with talent, hard work, emotionally intelligent handling of circumstances, and opportunities granted.

Figure 5.4
Modeling process, mimicking actual panel fabrication, allowed for more accurate study of precast shaping depth in relation to light. (2018) Credit: LMN Architects.

CTO career path

Cory Brugger, is an architect and designer. Just prior to the inter-view, Cory announced that he was leaving Morphosis and joining HKS as their new CTO:

When I first met with HKS the idea being discussed was for me to start up a LINE (Laboratory for INtensive Exploration) cluster in LA because they wanted to expand the reach of the group. Heath May (director and influence behind the creation of our HKS LINE) and I go back years. We've been chatting for a long time about joining forces somehow. And the right opportunity finally came up. When I met with Dan (Noble, HKS's CEO) he was like, no way, we want something bigger. As the conversation evolved, the one thing that came out is that there is a genuine interest to invest resources and time into innovation. The idea that sold the firm to me was their work on establishing a framework for responsible design. They showed me their internal chart for the five key project stakeholders, which includes Client/Users, Client/Capital, Co-Creators, Earth, and Community. This showed that they care beyond just the design of a building. It demonstrated a new level of professional and ethical responsibility that I haven't seen in many firms before, especially at our scale. That convinced me that their intentions were in the right place. Our values aligned in terms of what architecture could be. Now, we had to take a step back to define our path forward and leverage what they have in place already.

We've got all these initiatives that are spokes going out in their own directions. They all operate somewhat siloed. Everybody recognizes it and we all agree that creating synergy among the groups is our biggest opportunity for growth. We have some of the smartest people in the industry. A lot of back end information and expertise. So now we've got to figure out how to leverage our overlap in knowledge and process. Much of our initial work is really about process change. Some of the work will inevitably involve technology, but we need to look at it first and foremost as process change. If we're really looking at this as an innovation group, then we need to start rethinking how we establish success metrics and what tracking and assessing them means. There will be initiatives that fail or do not achieve the intended outcomes. It is part of pursuing innovation. After all progress is based upon experimentation. We'll need to learn how to deal with this. Some studios' culture already supports innovation initiatives. Office-wide? Not so much. That's to be expected, HKS is a large firm with well-established processes. Many of the younger staff are focused on pinnacle wins, and the need to carry the technology all the way through. There is a need to see everything perfectly executed. Which is great, but we need small wins too, and a lot of them to convince people that we're moving in the right direction. My first four months are discovery. I need to look at regions, to look at markets, to look at each of the offices. See what our strengths are. Establish what the median capability and proficiency is. HKS operates as one firm. So while individual offices work semi-independently, we tend to share expertise and resources firm-wide based on project, sector, and market need. Within that one firm mentality we have a need to define our median proficiency – see who's below and see who's above – and figure out what we can do better to support our staff and our projects. How do we maintain equilibrium in different market sectors and regions that may not have, nor need, that same expertise? We would like to have the ability to easily swap out staff so there is a global push to upskill our workforce.

I have so much to learn about the firm. I have standing meetings set up with HKS's Practice Technology group to help set the tone for when I come on board. I have a meeting set up with Heidi Dial HKS CIO (Mark Overton left right after I joined), Jim Whittaker who directs alternative delivery, and Ray Smith the director of technical resources, HKS's detailing group; Kirk Krueger our Director of Construction Services (CA services); Lean strategies group (Bernita Beikmann); and Workplace strategies group (Kate Davis, Place Performance – Jull Duncan). This group of people are the ones I am aiming to have a conversation with. They have strong groups, and they have direction. And now we're going to be spending a lot more time together focusing on an aligned vision. We've sat down to discuss our history. The work we have done in the past, looking at project delivery, and alternative uses or downstream uses for models beyond CD documentation. My first conversations with Dan were like: I want to talk to Alternative Delivery. I want to talk to Specifications. I want

Figure 5.5
The Eleventh rendering. (2018) Credit: Design Architect – Bjarke Ingels Group.

to talk to Legal. Everybody was like, wait, we're talking about technology. No, this is where everything has to be rooted. We need to look at both our ability as an office to deliver something new, and also what does it mean to Practice, to Liability, to how we write and sign contracts? To set the tone before coming on board, I met with Dan and Billy (Hinton, Director of Architecture) and they asked me what does a CTO at an architecture firm look like? I responded by giving them a 32-page document with every-thing from interactions with all the firm's work groups, different levels of organizational relationships, as well as why those orga-nizational relationships are important. I tried to focus on the idea of a CTO using the four quadrants from The Role of the CTO: Four Models for Success, *by Tom Berray. The underlying vision for the role was what we needed to establish. The two topics that I focused on were process and innovation. HKS has two ambitions. We want clients to come to us for landmark projects. So part of the push is to be recognized as a go-to design firm. The second ambition is that we want, through responsible design and innovation, to find a way to add value for all project stakeholders. To positively influence the industry and the built environment. What can we do differently? What kind of innovations can help us change the way we practice?*

Computationally Inclined Architect (CIA) covert career path

Ryan Cameron, Project Architect and Associate, DLR Group:

My first real introduction to design technology was with Maya 2006. It didn't have an x-ray mode and I realized you could create custom commands [much like AutoCAD] using the [Maya-Embedded Language] MEL scripts. I think it was 12 lines of code [trial and error], and it completely changed my experience in that program. Immersing myself at that level made me realize anything is possible.

Every five years I rebuild my entire skillset. It's painful. I sit down and say, the stuff I did last year, I want to blow it out of the water. It's a constant five-year rebuild. That's due more to the recession than anything. When I was in college – I graduated with an engineering degree in 2001, a B.Arch in 2006 (a year behind Nate Miller at University of Nebraska–Lincoln) – between January 2002 and 2006, I did a complete rebuild of everything. In 2002 I was still using CAD. In 2006, I was deep into Revit. By the recession of 2008, getting laid off in December 2010, I was deep into Revit, 3DsMax, Rhino, and Maya. I was winning a lot of awards and competitions because of those skills in that time frame between 2006–2010. That was another rebuild. After that layoff I had to gut and rebuild everything. I got into computer science quite a bit more. There were no jobs for me, so I knew I had to start creating my own something. I started with Architect Machines and building data management, and a data asset management tool that could be used by anybody because when I got laid off, I lost all of my models, the families, the scripts I built. Granted, some of it belonged to the firm that I worked for at the time so I had to rebuild everything from scratch. I'd hate for that to happen to anybody else. It was happening left and right. All of my college classmates were just getting laid off between 2009 and 2012. So, I thought, wouldn't it be nice if they had a resource where they could put all their files – not like RevitCity.com or FoodForRhino.com – and just have a tiny sliver of their true digital portfolio (not their online portfolio with rendered images and floor plans) but your tools portfolio, and to be able to put that in a safe place? Not just DropBox it but share it, and see what other people are making. That's where Architecture Machines came from. We developed apps and all kinds of things. I really started to getting into coding at that point. In 2014 I got into Arduino programming and sensor building. Then asked, how do I tie this in with what I am doing? It was, once again, a complete rebuild of my skillsets. My day-to-day became quad touchscreen monitors that come apart, get brought near me, touchscreen access to all of my data dashboards. That was the next step of skill rebuild.

Every few years I have an assessment of my skills and hard re-evaluation on what to drop and what to add. It's always painful dropping a skill you put four to five years into but realize you can only master so many at a time. Dropping AutoCAD created an opening for Revit. Dropping Sketchup created an opening for Rhino. I could go into any legacy program and do the minor task I need to in the program, then move onto my current data environment. Knowing that has helped me relax a little when rebuilding my skillset. I can't predict what that shift will be. I only know there will be a shift and to prepare now. I've already started my next rebuild schedule. So many mundane tasks are automatable in this field – truly automatable – and we'd be better off for it. Unfortunately, that rebuild isn't my usual hardware-mode, software-upgrade cycle. I'd like to include my kids in these tech adventures, too. My oldest has some interest in game development for mobile. Maybe it turns into a client-to-architect app that makes construction documents. Who knows? There's a lot of opportunities I see that keep me passionate.

Career-wise, if your goal is to rise in the organization then build that support and find a common language. For me, if it gets recognized, great. I'm also busy with running my own company and working with other businesses to help provide insight on technology. I love what I do at DLR Group but if I only wanted recognition I would have left long ago. Getting emails about how I helped someone has been more rewarding than climbing the corporate ladder. Design tech is viewed as a "tech position" still. How you change that view is up to the person in that role.

Computational BIM manager career path
Jordan Billingsley, Design Technology Specialist, Hord Coplan Macht:

When I was in grad school, some of my favorite classes were the more abstract and theory-based architecture classes, and for almost all of my projects, the feedback was, "There's no fault to your logic, there's no fault to your reasoning. Your drawings are just not developed enough." I didn't like working on the drawings as much. I liked telling the story, figuring out the logic behind a problem. So I only received markdowns for my renderings not being polished, or for not having enough drawings to point at. So, it was pretty consistent criticism. I always considered myself a Jack-of-all-Trades kind of person, and after I graduated it was a recession, so it was a good time for me to do my own thing. So I was doing entrepreneurial freelancing work under the Blackline umbrella. I did some freelance rendering and some freelance model making, and I leveraged some of those skills that I had learned while I was a student. I had a good background, a good mix of things. CERL taught me how to use Excel and database management really well, because everything is data with the army. And at Porter Athletic, I learned how to build really good parametric families, so both of those have roots in information. Then I got married and my wife accepted a job at Johns Hopkins, so that was the move out to Baltimore. And when I first moved out here, oddly enough I had never had an internship at an office, I had never been employed by an architecture firm, and I was actually very intimidated or cautious about working at a large firm. A multi-office, hundred person plus firm, that was what I considered large at the time, so I opted to work at a small firm when I first moved out here. And my reasoning was that I was already doing all aspects of my freelance work, and I didn't want to give up that kind of control. I didn't want to specialize at that time, or so I thought. At the small office that I ended up working for, I met a really good project manager who ended up taking me back to a much larger firm, HCM, so I was only at that small firm for maybe four months. And when I was recruited by this larger firm, they actually vaguely described it as Revit support, and I said, "Okay, that's fine, but I really want to still be focused on project work." But as I got more and more involved within the Revit processes, and them in general, because it extended past Revit pretty quickly, I just kept moving up and they wanted me to move into a BIM coordinator role for the firm. So, now I'm helping with four different office locations, and I never thought that I would enjoy problem-solving as much. Now I'm trying to get only put onto smaller projects, or really problematic *projects, and mostly just staying on the BIM side of the work. I don't know if that's a direct route or even good advice, but that's the way that I came to my position.*

Technology consultant career path

Ana Garcia Puyol, Director of User Experience and Integration at IrisVR:

I studied architecture in Spain and during my fifth year of architecture school, I went to study in Carbondale, Illinois. I spent my fifth year of architecture school at Southern Illinois University (SIU). Even though they had very little technology and it wasn't a full-on computational design education, they did have laser cutters and a CNC and then some of the students were learning Grasshopper. These were things that I had never seen or heard of while I was studying in Spain. Looking back, of course, and connecting the dots, how everything turned out makes sense. In October of 2010, I went back home (to Spain) to finish my studies and, randomly enough, a Generative Components (Bentley) workshop had been organized at my university. Don't ask me why . . . I signed up for it and it was a little expensive at the time, but it was a great investment. It was so fun. In addition to that, for my thesis project as part of the six-year professional degree I was part of, I decided to learn Grasshopper on my own.

It didn't end there. Upon graduation, I was set on learning more about digital design and fabrication and how to make very difficult things because it represented a challenge. So I applied to grad school and ended up going to the Harvard Graduate School of Design to earn a Master in Design Studies with a concentration in Technology. I'm one of the very few people who can say that my degree, my education, was in design technology. It's a very new thing. The program, it's now perhaps 15 years old? It was great. I did a lot of work with robots, with the ABBs. I did a lot of work with CAD/CAM in general. Of course a lot of laser cutting, 3D printing, and then a lot of BIM. I also took a class at MIT with Zach Kron and Dennis Shelden. Dennis Shelden at that time was at Gehry Technologies and Zach Kron was at Autodesk. He started teaching us Dynamo, which was in its early state. It was funny because I said to him, "Hey, Zach, I can't do this thing," and he'd be like, "You just found a fault (or bug) for us, thanks." They would fix it and I would continue doing my work. And then, of course, I got super excited about all of this and there were only two companies that I wanted to work for when I graduated: CASE Inc. and TT CORE Studio. So I came to New York and built my portfolio just for these firms. I interviewed with both. I had met Jonatan Schumacher briefly before. I interviewed with him on a Tuesday and on Friday he offered me a job.

Note

1 Ed Catmull and Amy Wallace, *Creativity, Inc.: Overcoming the Unseen Forces That Stand in the Way of True Inspiration*, Random House, 2014.

Chapter 6

Engaging (and retaining) Superusers

Engaging and retaining Superusers really has to do with the proper care and feeding of Superusers: how do you keep them, and keep them from leaving for richer pastures?

Technology specialists in AEC are a special breed, and engagement is about retaining these valued employees. The usual go-to tactics – an attaboy/attagirl, or gift card – just won't cut it. Engaging and retaining Superusers involves nurturing the 10 Cs, the soft skills, mindsets, attitudes, and hard skills possessed by every Superuser.

The chapter opens with the ways firms keep things moving, interesting, and relevant for design technology specialists. Next, we look at when Superusers leave AEC for startups and other industries, why they leave startups for AEC, and how firms compete with these startups for Superusers, and concludes with a look at the training and upskilling of Superusers.

Where is the world going, and how can we avoid being eaten alive by software and robots?

A group of LMN Architects employees were recently reading and discussing R. Susskind and D. Susskind's book, *The Future of the Professions: How Technology Will Transform the Work of Human Experts*. LMN Architects Principal Stephen Van Dyck was reading the book, and was convinced that everybody in his company needed to read it. Van Dyck says:

> At a cursory glance, as a leader in this business it may seem really problematic to have your staff grapple with this future – that perhaps professional services might be automated in the near future. But I see it the other way around, which is: how can

you not have your staff think about this problem? These are ideas that everyone in our company should be thinking about every day. I want people to constantly question, ask how can we make everything we do more efficient and better, to free up our time to do the most critical activities that only architects can?

With all the work and deadlines firms have to contend with, how do important group discussions such as this come about? Van Dyck explains:

> In one of our early planning sessions, I mentioned somewhat glibly, "Oh, I'm reading this book about the future of work which has blown my mind into smithereens. This is really incredible stuff, and I think it's really important for us to think about together." The group seemed really intrigued by the topic, so I asked, "What do you guys think about just doing a book club? Anybody who is interested can come." I thought it was important to have this be disconnected from official office business. Other than the office providing office space, where we just meet in our flex area after hours. I personally go buy chips and wine. Others bring snacks and stuff too. We do it on weekday evenings between 6:00 and 8:00 p.m. The intent is not to make it an office-sanctioned event, but to make it more a conversation among friends about a really important topic, which is: where is the world going, and how can we not be eaten alive by robots?

Or software? "Or software," agrees Van Dyck. He continues:

> So I put a post on our Intranet and said, "Hey, we're going to start a book club offline. Anybody who wants to join, let me know, and we'll figure out how to do it." And 37 people responded! I was blown away by the interest. So we split up into two groups to make the conversations more manageable. We discussed the first half of the book in two sessions, last week and the week before, and we're going to do the second half when I get back from my travels in a week or two. We call ourselves the LMN Existentialists. Of course that started the wheels turning in my mind, and we've got a whole bunch of other books and articles on tap. To some degree we function like a support group, because this is a

really existentialist crisis that we're in. We as a profession, as members of society, we have to grapple with this topic. What is the world like when machines can do a lot of our work better than we can?

The group is also an informal brainstorming session. The conversations are a way for us to think proactively. All of this is to some degree, formally or informally, makes its way into how we structure the future of our firm. It's just a slightly unexpected way to do it. It's a new way of cultivating strategy with our staff to help make sure that we're positioned well.

This is just one of many ways firms are going out of their way to engage – and retain – the very people who help them succeed. It leverages one of the greatest advantages that a firm has – that it is not just a confluence of individuals, but a collaborative group with shared interests and outcomes. Van Dyck says:

I believe that we're all better off talking about the existential crisis together. It just goes back to some basic human stuff. Sometimes, it's hard to talk about difficult things. And this is a difficult subject. It's a hard conversation to have, but there's really good stuff that can come out of it. That's my hope, to be proactive about things that people are really scared about. The more we can be smart about it and think about the bad and the good, the better chance we stand to fare well in the future. It's an experiment. I don't know how it's going to turn out. You can ask me this question in five years. How did it go?

Engaging Superusers

Today, it is important to keep our best people engaged in the work they are performing. And from a management standpoint, it is equally important, where possible, to align an individual's professional development with the business goals of the firm. "I try to equally get them to understand the pros and cons of being in a role like this," says CannonDesign CTO Hilda Espinal. She continues:

I try to give him or her every sensible chance to be exposed to as much of a variety of opportunities as are available. I love to give them the spotlight and step aside and see what they can do and perform and deliver and contributing to their professional development. It's like, OK, is this where you wanted to go? Here is your chance. I always tell everybody, "listen, if we're doing our job right, two or three years down the road we will render ourselves obsolete, you have to be OK with that and enjoy change, evolving is the recipe to success."

Those conversations are happening a lot, because not only am I evolving myself, but I'm evolving with my crew and they are evolving themselves.

A lot of the answer has to do with my leadership style. Without, hopefully, sounding arrogant, I've developed an eye for identifying what folks love to do and what they can do, which often go hand in hand. So as long as it is in line with our vision, I try to align their development with business goals. It is also important to have regular communications and do path-correction, whenever possible. Frank feedback and check-in points, I find, always help.

Keeping things moving for design technologists

Today's professionals need to always be learning and growing professionally. But sometimes there's the perception that the firm itself is what stands in the way of design technologists feeling like they

Figure 6.1 Shane Burger in the Woods Bagot VR lounge. Woods Bagot developed an app for iOS and Android devices that allow clients, using a compatible lens, to walk through their designs on their own phones. (2018) Credit: James and Karla Murray.

can continually learn and grow. From an employee retention stand-point, this can cause firm leaders trouble, in terms of always having to keep things interesting. Shane Burger, Principal and Global Leader of Technical Innovation at Woods Bagot says:

It is definitely an issue. I give people a lot of room to learn, because, for me, I'm not counting hours. Everybody fills out timesheets, but I kind of don't care. If you get the work done, and it's good, and you want to spend part of a Wednesday afternoon learning something new, great. If you want to go off and teach at Columbia, Pratt, or somewhere else, great. Doing so keeps people creatively and intellectually stimulated in their work, beyond just the project work that they are doing.

These things do pose a problem, because firms have to maintain a relatively fast pace. Burger continues:

The thing that we've run into at Woods Bagot, and part of what caused Brian Ringley and Andrew Heumann to leave, the speed of the gears of the design technology team were going at a much higher pace. Yet, when it hit the mechanizations of an 850-person global company, that size of a ship is hard to turn. It's harder to pivot. We're doing really well, and compared to our peers are doing really well. But sometimes it isn't quite up to speed with keeping things moving for people. Because of that, ultimately, if you have a pretty big critique of the profession in general, or at least the business of architecture, then that's not going to keep you as interested.

It's been less about interesting projects. I'm a believer that a group of amazing people can take a mediocre project and turn it into an amazing one. It doesn't have to, by default, be a tower with a huge budget, an amazing client, with an art museum at the base. That's not where you're going to get an amazing project from. The biggest issue we run into, coming from retention of really good staff, has more to do with boring things like management, project pipeline, and diversity of project types. Keeping that stuff going. Keeping a diverse set of interesting things going on in the studio. It's been less about *I got to work on an amazing tower for three years*. And it's been more about career advancement and promotion.

When Superusers leave AEC for startups, and when they leave startups for AEC

Inspired by – and having to compete with – startup culture, firms are offering design technologists opportunities to conduct research and innovate – a win-win for both employees and for firms. TT CORE has an R&D program open to all staff, which allows anyone to submit a proposal. According to Hiram Rodriguez, Computational Design Group Leader at Thornton Tomasetti:

> If they get it they will be funded for that project, which is great because we are not the only group trying to come up with content but you have others outside of the group create some of that content.
>
> It is crucial to have an R&D program if you want the company to explore new technologies or workflows. Not only are you allowing your staff to further their knowledge, you are creating new value for the company as a whole. In terms of TT CORE, we have been doing more development in the last year, but we maintain a healthy ecosystem of project support, training, internal research, and outreach. For example, having focus group discussions about tool development is something that we're starting to do more of, and remains key to building tools that can reach a broad range of people.

The AEC industry is increasingly losing computational designers, design technologists, and similar specialists to other industries. Another trend is that there are people in other industries, e.g. in startups, that end up taking a significant cut in salary to work for an AEC firm. They're willing to take the cut to work less with spreadsheets and more with their hands, e.g. coming up with digital prototypes for projects and find that to be very fulfilling.

Why do design technologists choose to stay in the AEC industry? What career opportunities are there for computational designers who remain? Why don't they leave AEC firms for an allegedly more lucrative career at WeWork, Katerra, Autodesk, or Disney? What are the opportunities and liabilities of staying, in terms of design technologists' career development? "For my twelve people, I always think there's tons of opportunity for them," says Dan Anthony, Design Computation Leader at NBBJ. He continues:

Part of the nature of our industry is constant change. For people, for their professional careers. I've watched a lot of good colleagues go for different reasons. And I've watched a lot of good people come for great reasons, too. What I have found is that their instincts are usually correct.

Concerning the liabilities, "A lot of times they are not being utilized to their fullest potential, and they go somewhere else to explore that potential," says Anthony. He continues:

That's OK. I would love to keep people in that spot, designers who are computationally savvy. But it's a hard space to be in. Because you either don't want to become too specialized, or don't feel like you get to express it enough in the work that you do. That's the hardest part about that role. For them, as long as they try to maintain that balance, they are actually very, very valuable.

Just months after stating these words, Anthony himself moved on from NBBJ, joining a software startup building design tools to power the Superusers at construction and architecture firms – like the one he left.

Superusers are understandably hard to come by. "Made even more difficult by the fact that we have now totally different kinds of companies snatching up our great talent, verticals like Katerra and WeWork," says Van Dyck. Architecture and engineering firms, as well as construction companies, have seen good people leave for a startup. LMN Architects is no exception. "Oh, yeah," says Van Dyck:

If you spend any time at the WeWork headquarters, what you see is a very large operation with a lot of people in the C Suite, and a glitzy start-up atmosphere. In their current state, they are certainly optimized to lure some of the best design technologists over there. But there is a lot unknown about where they're able to take their model. I think the jury's out on that.

I'm really curious to see what happens with them, if this allure stays for the technologically inclined architects. I think the big scale of what they're doing with this typology of building and the way that they approach design as an integrated part of their business model is awesome. I'm really fascinated to see where it goes and the things they learn. I'm just not sure it's going to remain as alluring to those talents as it is now.

But are these startups in the same industry as AEC? "No," says Van Dyck. He continues:

They're in the same industry as many of our clients. They're operating in the world of academic campuses and large real-estate firms. Now, they're beginning to offer models of facilities and operations to all kinds of companies, which is really fascinating. It doesn't preclude us. It's totally possible that there will be a project where WeWork would really benefit from hiring us. I think of them as a future client.

When people decide not to leave or disband, or not go to another company or industry, what is it about what we do that keeps them from jumping ship? According to Van Dyck:

It's the idea of being immersed in a breadth of design work that elevates the social experience. That's our focus. That's the outcome we help create. It's the experience we help shape across a wide range of project types. At LMN we don't have any studios, which means we all work on all sorts of project typologies. You might be working on a convention center today, and you might be working on a performing arts center or a pedestrian bridge in a month's time. That diversity of design expertise means diversity of perspective. It's critical to our outcomes and our ability to solve problems in new ways. Another important element for us is the fact that as a young designer you can have a lot of impact on projects and working process. Our teams are generally small. Our projects range in size from small to large. And they're all quite different in function. You're not going to be stuck designing housing within a specific supply chain all the time. You're not going to be spending the rest of your career maximizing the efficiency of office space. So in a nutshell, we offer a broader experience for an architect while simultaneously maintaining a constant curiosity about how we can reinvent our services and process. I think that's what attracts people to LMN.

The other side of this is, what attracts people to those places? "It's their explicit objective to disrupt a market," says Van Dyck. "That concept of disruption is important to people. People want to feel like they're contributing to something meaningful and new." As they do currently at WeWork and Katerra. "Exactly," says Van Dyck:

> People really want to know that they're part of something that is growing. The perception is that there's growth in disruption, which is often true. It certainly is true now with those two companies. I would argue that LMN also offers that sense of growth and disruption. We don't have a pro-forma that creates a potential stock valuation of whatever billion dollars, but we are reimagining our role and approach at different scales constantly. Whether it's our design process or how we collaborate with our partners or how we engage in post-occupancy work. All of that is disrupting the status quo of traditional architectural service, we're just not explicitly branding it as disruption.
>
> That's really the difference between those choices, working for a firm like LMN or a vertical like WeWork. Do you want to work for an industry disrupter with a very narrow focus? A vertical has to remain very tightly focused on what that thing does. Their business model right now, it is dependent on filling office space. Their revenue and their funding is based upon how much office space and members they have. It's the T-shaped question, do you want to be really good at one thing, dial that in and do a ton of research about it? Or do you want to remain somebody with a broad reach that is able to affect a more diverse set of problems? The answer for me is being broad and horizontal. I really embrace the breadth of the architect's role to be a great generalist and orchestrator to solve complicated social needs.

As a transdisciplinary practice, KieranTimberlake has a number of people who could be working outside of architecture and perhaps making more money. Partner Matthew Krissel says:

> But they are passionate about the built environment. And rightfully so, many people still believe that architects have a meaningful impact on society, that the built environment is not neutral, it can have a profound impact and it can enrich or diminish the human

experience. Increasingly people are much more conscious about what they do and the impact they can have as criteria for their careers.

Shane Burger got into a conversation with Federico Negro, Head of Design at WeWork about this. "He commented that he was doing critiques at one of the universities and had people coming up to him and talking about potential positions at WeWork," says Burger. He continues:

The point these people were making was, all of their friends were going into software development companies. It's arguably sexier and more lucrative. It's a quicker pace. You produce things that get out there a little faster. That said, this only appeals to certain people. Maybe it's something they do for a while, but there's still something really impressive about buildings and creating spaces, especially ones that have a very personal impact on people within an urban environment, such as New York. Not all architecture is timeless, but it's a lot closer than creating an app. There's still a strong interest, and we are finding some people who, yes, they can go out there and work for a Google. One of the software developers I am interviewing right now could go out and work for Autodesk, Google, or similar company. But he actually doesn't

Figure 6.2
Our industry's approach to the digital and delivery of data in the built environment needs to stop looking like a spreadsheet and more like prototyping with sensors. (2011) Credit: Smartgeometry.

want to. He wants to stay a little more close to the problems. And see something actually come from his work beyond the software that he created. He wants to see it used for something. That's what's of interest to him.

Woods Bagot is finding a lot more back-and-forth with this. Burger continues:

What we've had in the past are architects who are interested in developing programs to do their work, to make plug-ins or Grass-hopper definitions. Some of them have gotten so good that they meet the caliber of what you'd find out there in the industry to work for a software company. So they decided *I might as well cross over there and try that for a while*. I'm not sure that that shift is going to increase in velocity. We're always going to have some of that. We're competing with other architecture firms, and we're competing with software developers. We're also finding an increasing amount of people in the AEC lifecycle of projects, or the whole ecosystem, that are seeing increasing importance of these skills. That's of course who WeWork's hiring. Airbnb are hiring people who do this kind of stuff. Lots of different software companies and contractors. There's a significant amount of the real estate market in New York that are building up their own tools similar to (3D web app) Envelope City and such. What we're seeing is a lot more people interested in the skills of a programmer, but also someone who thinks critically like an architect. There's a great combination in those skills and we're finding a lot of other businesses in the larger built environment ecosystem that want to bring a lot more of that stuff in-house.

Prior to coming to Woods Bagot, Burger worked at Grimshaw. He stayed in architecture, in AE, and continues to work in this space and make inroads, leveraging the tools for the greater good. What is in Burger's DNA that enables him to persevere in, and not abandon, the AEC industry, while others leave it for greener pastures? Burger says:

I am still really fascinated with buildings and spaces. I'm still fascinated with the creative act of collaboration. The reference for me still comes back to the years I spent, when I was much younger, playing in bands. And what it meant to collaboratively create something. That process gets my blood going – I am so excited by it – and it keeps me going.

Dan Anthony worked in tech before coming to design and architecture. He admits:

At the time, I wasn't the most technical of people. I wasn't writing the code day to day for our product. I was managing products and designing what the feature sets should be for certain things. The reason I got into design was exactly that: the outcome. I wanted to understand how to lead a more creative practice that wasn't simply the fulfillment of some other things. It occurred to me if I didn't have those design skills I would never have them. I wanted to acquire design skills, then went out and got them. I, too, took the pay hit.

Could another reason people stick with the AEC industry be financial – the perception of *sunk costs*? "The cynical answer is 'Well, you already paid for your degree and you started a family, and you just don't feel it's worth the risk of trying something new,' but I don't think that's it actually," says Brian Ringley, Senior Researcher at WeWork. He continues:

I'm not actually a cynic. I think it's funny to open with that and it's probably a little bit like it's not easy to switch once you're inside. Now, I'm in too deep. What is that called? The sunk cost fallacy. People have a genuine passion for architecture. People

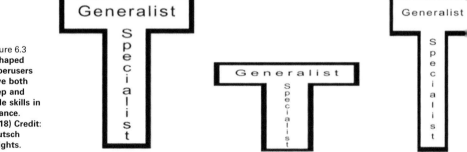

Figure 6.3
T-shaped
Superusers
have both
deep and
wide skills in
balance.
(2018) Credit:
Deutsch
Insights.

who are in architecture really, really love architecture. That's not necessarily true of say the tax industry. Well, maybe it is.

I will say I'm tired of the people who are in architecture proper bitching about it. It's a little tiresome, but I also understand those frustrations and I feel lucky to have all these opportunities to continually try new things. I myself, I'm still doing architecture, it's just at scale and it's vertically integrated in a way that is not commonly found in practice, because I am fascinated by cities and by buildings. I remember it happened to me at a pretty young age. It's really comical to think about, I used to be obsessed with ranch homes when I was in high school. I loved these old 1960s drawings of these cheesy ranch houses. I feel like it's ultimately just a passion for the built environment, and no matter how [expletive] things seem to them, I think that's still where they want to be, and they still want to work to improve it.

Competing with startups for Superusers

Is one solution to try to compete with the startups – including vertically integrated companies interested in owning the entire project pipeline – for the best people? Increasingly, one doesn't need to leave architecture and engineering firms to experience the advantages of startups. "There's no doubt that a lot of wonderful things can happen when you control and define the whole design to construction lifecycle," admits Matthew Krissel. He elaborates:

I like how these firms can define the whole design and construction lifecycle, and I hope this kind of focused pressure can become real agents of change. No doubt, when you try and solve all the challenges across everything that architecture and construction may touch, it's too much and too interconnected to take it all on at once. I believe these types of practices can make real change by taking on smaller pieces and stair step the progress and examples for everyone's benefit.

At the same time, it's great that a single designer, with a job in hand, can open a design practice and complete a project. They don't need lots of capital or a network of relationships to get started. This keeps an entrepreneurial version of a design practice viable and relevant. I also like how a practice like ours, a design and research practice, can take on so many different things all at the same time. We are not held back by any one element of the vertical chain or an area of focus critical to the operation. Whether it's making software, designing a house, mapping the behavior and environmental factors, a large office building or an esoteric academic building, when we see projects we want to take on we can do it. We can scale and adapt our business model, contacts, design process, deliverables, our partnerships, and our interest to almost anything. I believe there is still lots of space and many forms for a design practice to take and thrive within. Some we have seen before and others [are] yet [to be] invented. I wouldn't want to see a contraction of this dynamism where everyone looks to become vertically oriented. I would, however, like to see a more coordinated effort across these scales to shape mutually beneficial areas of how we teach design and architecture, advance fabrication, construction, delivery, and operations of buildings and how we shape clients to be more aspirational and motivated to deliver meaningful projects. Architecture, construction, and operations all bear great responsibility but also opportunity. Performance and poetics are not mutually exclusive, rather their fusion is imperative at a time when the built environment must give more than it takes.

Are there similarities in what an AE firm like NBBJ does with the work that WeWork, or anyone in the co-working real estate space, does? "Yes and no," says Dan Anthony:

You can imagine some of the techniques they use being very interesting. WeWork is expanding from a core area of putting butts in seats in standardized yet attractive spaces. Filling the seats. Their goal is to fill those seats at the highest price most often in as many spaces in as many buildings as possible. That is real estate. What's curious is that they have started to develop techniques to capture the corporate market. Creating more specialized spaces. Which is about putting a company in a WeWork building. So they're offering them their design services. It has to start from a very numbers-driven, top-down approach. How do we get as many companies in these standardized spaces? What does the space need to be to suit their needs but also be really easy to roll out? In my role I'm interested in the techniques they use. If the scope and scale of their work allows them to create something powerful and useful, but they hold on to them and they're proprietary, that is a market edge that could eventually bleed into the design space. The risk for us, whether AE or AEC, is we'll probably have the edge in terms of design and specialization. Making spaces that are unique for our clients.

For our client, we have a different attitude. Our goal isn't to fill seats as often as possible, but maybe to design the building that works best for their business. We're interested in human performance in that way. We want to think about spaces that don't just meet the bottom line but also to help them to do their best work. Sometimes that means having some waste. We have more space than we need because we want to accommodate flexibility and choice. The question I have is: How does a company like WeWork understand the general human conception of what a workplace should be like? Do they own that IP? Do they make a tool that we can all use? These are big questions. These are all things that we can imitate in a way, but also have a different tactic. On companies such as WeWork or Autodesk: We're just going to keep on collecting data until it tells us something.

Brian Ringley concurs that WeWork, for all its ambition, currently has a more narrow focus. "At WeWork, we have huge ambitions," says Ringley. He continues:

But part of what allows for scaling and vertical integration is that relatively constrained design space, it's that specialization in workplace and the ability to systematize that, and also an often under-looked fact is just redeveloping existing properties and how sustainable and quick that can be. There are so many underutilized spaces in the world, and yet the default real estate mode is buy a piece of land, have an architect create a core and shell building as tall as possible, and then sell that. They just keep doing that and you're never actually looking at the demand. It's all just pure speculation.

Training and upskilling Superusers

How do Superusers learn and stay relevant? Lunch & Learns, and earning continuing education learning units, don't always cut it. Are

Figure 6.4
Technical
façade draw-
ings. (2018)
Credit:
Nathan
Bataille, Pratt
GAUD.

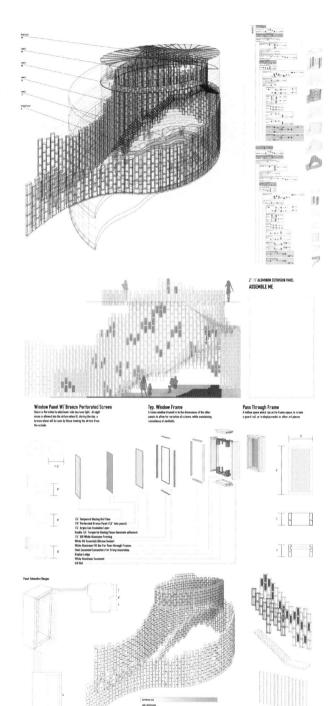

firms responsible for preparing employees for the future? If so, how would they go about it. DLR Group's Ryan Cameron strongly recommends a skill rebuild approach:

> You should rebuild yourself every three, four, five, six, or seven years. I believe Frank Lloyd Wright had that advice. A few years ago I discovered that Gensler has their own in-house lab, and Gensler University, where employees can put in time to learn software or something else and the firm says, "OK, let's go do that." What if we applied something similar to that but also meshed it with something similar to a one- or two-year development league for NBA between high school and professional basketball league, that gets you substantially more prepared for all the actual stuff you're going to run into? Professional basketball's not just a physical game; it's a mental game. There's all kinds of trash-talking, things you have to be ready for. Otherwise you're just going to get mentally broken down.
>
> The exact same thing is true with architecture. If you're not going to be mentally ready, career-ready, hands-ready, skill-ready, you're really going to flop your first year, because it is such a hard thing to prepare for and overcome. If there was something like an Architect Development League (ADL) where you took a year between college and practice, the firm you're going to work for, that would be interesting. You could have all the big firms say, "This is our definition of what that is. We'll pay for it. We'll buy a building somewhere and that's where people go." As we start to discover who's the most talented, we start to fight over them. Because that's how it happens now. Your smaller firms, they'd have their own cultured development league that's fit for their style of play. So for the people who want to go to a big firm, there's the development league avenue. People who want to join, work, or stay at a boutique-type firm, there's a development league for that.

One way to further develop design technology specialists is to equate firm engagement with opportunities to learn and grow professionally. "There are only a few colleges that have a computational design program," says Jordan Billingsley. "I believe Columbia had the first that began in the 1970's." Others include Harvard GSD, Stevens Institute, and Georgia Tech, among others. Billingsley continues:

If you don't have a graduate from one of these programs, the best way to develop aspiring employees is to give them an unlimited conference budget and an unlimited expense account for learning resources. If there is pushback to unlimited budgets, I give the example of Virgin and Netflix, where they have given their employees unlimited vacation yet there has not been any paid time off abuse because employees are invested in their work projects and feel fulfilled and supported. With regards to unlimited conference and professional development budgets, I don't even think it is possible to be abused, because the more conferences you go to, the more networks you create, the better informed you are about everything that's going on in that space. Personally, whenever I go to a conference, I come away so stimulated that I have enough work for at least three months. As I become more of an expert in my field, lectures may become less valuable but the network I have built will continue to drive me.

It's all about finding ways to keep employees engaged. Billingsley encourages firms to open source their technology developments under a creative commons license. He's observed that most design technology specialists are self-taught, learning from free online communities, and sees a strong desire to give back to these communities. Firms that limit employee communication with online peers out of concern of protecting intellectual property, he believes, are stifling their own potential. Billingsley says:

I want to emphasize conferences, being able to work from home like I'm doing right now. Also, open source and firms creating their own tools. Almost everybody who is a computational designer, or works in computational BIM, design technology specialists, is getting their education for free via these blogs and forums and other sources. So, when they start to develop tools, or even if they're building off other tools, a firm shouldn't feel protective about that, because by releasing it or making it open source, as long as it doesn't have company information in it, that tool is going to naturally evolve into something so much better. As someone who wants to automate things, I don't want to worry about how do we protect this? That's one thing that I really don't want to care about. I know that might not be popular, but in terms of letting a design technology person be creative, you don't want to add more constraints.

Billingsley is the chair of his firm's design technology committee. When he first joined the Design Technology Committee (DTC) the monthly meetings addressed a single issue. "I found that technology sectors were outpacing our decision-making process," says Billingsley. Instead of increasing the frequency of meetings he decided to define seven technology sectors, or disciplines, and create specialist roles responsible for presenting succinct reports at each meeting. The seven technology disciplines are ABCDEFG; Automation, BIM, Content, Digital visualization, Early energy analysis, Fabrication, and General information technology. Billingsley explains:

> The way the committee was structured before was that it attacked a single issue at each monthly meeting. They'd ask, what did we do well this month, what did we not do well this month? What technology should we be looking at? Should we buy a new 3D printer? Should we get VR goggles? And each one of those were a separate meeting. For the first year, I continued running things that way, but I found that I was basically leading

Figure 6.5
UISOM rehearsal room swarms are a sculptural acoustic reflector system that doesn't obstruct the experience of the room's tall ceiling height. (2018) Credit: LMN Architects.

129

every meeting and doing all this research and we weren't moving fast enough for how big of a firm that we were. So what I've done is I've restructured our committee to be in seven disciplines. The seven groups are easy to remember because it's ABCDEFG. At every meeting, we meet once a month, we have seven reports that are five minutes long each. It works well.

One reason Billingsley diversified is he felt if he was ever hit by a bus everything would stop. "We needed to diversify and get more people involved, and also I needed to stop being the one who runs all of these meetings." He continues:

Right now we're in a transition period where I still have to set up all the slides, I have to set all of the goals, and sometimes I even rehearse the talking points for everybody. I might prepare entire slides for a certain section and give it to somebody else and say, "Okay, I want you to do this just for presentation purposes. I want a different face to be up there other than mine." I'm getting better at not micromanaging and just handing projects off. But also, other people need a framework for them to plug themselves into. Right now it's just about to take off.

Meeting is one thing, but getting the word out and making sure people are learning is another. Billingsley recognizes that dissemination of information is a problem that everyone grapples with. His firm records their DTC meetings and has placed members on active and non-active statuses, where active members are involved with development efforts whereas non-active member contributions are more advisory. Both groups, he assures, have access to recordings and help with awareness campaigns when developments are unveiled to the entire firm.

Part three
Managing and leading Superusers

Chapter 7

The career path not taken

The Superuser risk journey

The career paths of Superusers vary, but they do have commonalities. Challenges facing Superusers include how to keep one's hands on the technology, or on the building design, while minimizing the management of people. Others accept the role of managing people, budget, and schedule as an inevitable part of becoming a firm leader. How they handle and resolve career challenges and opportunities goes a long way to predict their rise within organizations.

In this chapter we'll look at the qualifications for career advancement of design technology specialists, including leveraging your talent for technology on building design projects, leveraging your architect status for a role in technology, and leveraging your talent for technology in managing people. No matter the specific roles they play, this chapter looks at how Superusers become the next generation of the profession, and looks at what stands in their way: the career risk journey of design technology specialists. Computational designers, by not following the traditional path, take on a lot of risks career-wise, and the professional trajectory becomes more of a risk journey rather than a career path. No matter the specific roles they play, this chapter looks at how Superusers become the next generation of the profession, and looks at what stands in their way: the career risk journey of design technology specialists. Finally, we'll look extensively at the career provenance of Superusers – including emerging, mid-career, and firm leaders; the IT path, BIM manager path, and internal consultant role – through career path case studies.

It is surprising to some that many design technologists and computational designers don't have a background in computer science or technology, but are instead former actors, playwrights, graphic designers, painters, or sculptors. "It is, for the most part, our group has as a variety of individuals with different backgrounds,

Figure 7.1
Navigating
from tradi-
tional titles
to emerging
roles. (2018)
Credit:
Jordan
Billingsley.

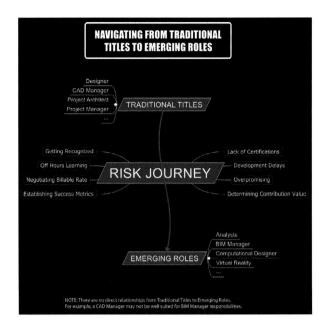

ranging from the arts to computer science," says Thornton Tomasetti Computational Design Group Leader Hiram Rodriguez. He
continues:

Computation Designer is a new emerging role, one that I believe
has the potential to create a major shift in the future of the AEC
industry. The key to getting the shift going would be to keep the
diversity with these groups which will yield better products,
workflows, and solutions.

I have an idea where the next steps are for someone within this
role. However, it is such a new role for the AEC industry that we
need to develop a comprehensive path for future computational
designers. In terms of our group, we have internal reviews and we
discuss career paths, which helps formulate this role within TT and
TT CORE. The role will change as technology changes, but we need
to be aware of what the tools are that are necessary to develop a
comprehensive role. Even within TT CORE we have several roles,
from Application Developer, Integration Engineer, and Computational Designer. I am sure the roles will get normalized or standardized within a few years; many firms are adopting the concept
because they see a benefit to automation.

Rodriguez's background is architecture, but he started as an art major where he focused in mix media arts and photography, which he still engages in from time to time. He says:

My introduction to the arts was crucial to think outside the box when solving some of the current computation problems we face today in our practice. In the AEC industry, we are always trying to solve problems and come up with noble ways of connecting the dots, and that is not easy if you do not have some level of curiosity and some level of understanding current technologies.

Is it up to schools, or the profession, to decide whether things get normalized in terms of where design technology specialists – *Superusers* – get their career start? Rodriguez says:

That's a question that has to be rooted back into education, right? Does the school then teach the new architects to integrate computational design as a new practice? The school that I went to was really invested in teaching Grasshopper and Python. The introduction for me was through school and I loved it. That is where I think the role comes in. If you normalize it and you just call it design, then in the future it will just be part of the industry. But it comes back to the institutions trying to teach those skills.

If one is inculcated into learning Grasshopper in school, they're naturally going to be looking to solve Grasshopper type problems – using computational thinking – or at least solve problems with the tools that they're familiar with and comfortable with, and enjoy using in the field. That's one way to normalize things. "That's the way drafting was normalized when it was part of the school curriculum, different times call for different skill adoptions," says Rodriguez. He continues:

So you'd learn how to use a T-square and a bunch of different types of pencils. It's crucial to have that kind of practice embedded in the architectural students, but it's crucial to teach them about new ways of thinking about solving problems through computational software. Maybe, we can think about volume, space, and proportions through computational tools.

According to a recent DesignIntelligence survey, only 50% of school curriculums are introducing students to new technologies,[1] creating a have/have-not situation for schools, and eventually, for emerging professionals and their firms.

Qualifications for career advancement

Nobody, right now, can anticipate what he or she will be doing in five to ten years. Most design technologists and computational designers haven't had a conversation in their office about their future, and don't have a clear idea of what that future is, so technology specialists must take it upon themselves to set goals with senior leadership, says Jordan Billingsley. He continues:

> There are no established metrics to measure their development, no certifications, no licenses – no badges of honor to recognize accomplishments and contributions. Design Technology specialists are often undervalued because their primary goal is to identify and eliminate "pain points" before they become systemic, i.e. the end user may never know how much effort went into solving a problem that would have plagued their project without a particular tool, workflow, or execution plan. Because efforts are undervalued, design technology specialists take on a lot of risk to develop their skills and it is certainly a labor of love often spending nights and weekends watching YouTube videos, following forums, and reading their RSS feeds.

So, is there a future for what Superusers are doing in and for their organizations? "Sadly, like all people who push the new, it's not even a real job title that's recognized in many firms," says Billingsley. He continues:

> We don't really have any good metrics for, "What did you do this year? What do you want to do this next year?" And even when we build a tool that clearly solves a pressure point or a pain point, or solves a problem that's been troubling people, there's not an accurate value that's been assigned to it. So if I design a tool that makes it possible so that you no longer have to do something that was a huge pain, like consulting coordination. We created some workflows that made it seamless for whenever a consultant has

their drawing sheets, it comes into our template. So that clearly has value to it. It clearly saved an hour, at least, for every project and every time you do a transmittal. But it's not valued appropriately, unfortunately. One is recognizing value within the firm, and two is you do have to set up goals so that they can achieve it.

Computational designers take on a lot of risks, as Billingsley explains:

Because, often, the way that they learn is outside of the firm, so they're spending their nights and weekends watching YouTube tutorials or going through 50 blogs through their Feedly, like I did.
Or lots of external training or paying for their own training in the very beginning stages, if that role doesn't exist, which it didn't at my firm. So they're taking a lot of risk that way. They also take a lot of risk in saying that they're not going to follow the traditional path. So, even when the firm does recognize, "Okay, you've been doing a lot of good work. I know you've been doing this outside of work a lot, we're going to protect a little bit of time for you." That's a really good scenario, by the way. If you get to that stage, you're considered to be valued, finally, in your organization. But, that value seems to have this invisible cap. We don't really know where it's at because you can't get licensed in computational design, you can't get LEED certification in computational

Known Career Paths	Untested Career Paths	New Roles
Project Manager	Design Technology Director	Manager Of Specialists
Project Architect	Design Technologist/ Computational BIM	Specialist
Project Designer	Computational Designer	Designer

Figure 7.2
On a career path, can a specialist become a principal? (2018) Credit: Deutsch Insights.

design, you can't get any of these nice little badges that traditional architects get. So, it's a lot of risk, and we need to make sure that we're valuing it, and people within your organization need to set up goals at performance evaluations, and that needs to be design technologist specialist-led, so they need to ask, "What do you want to do this year and why?" And just be supportive of it. And if they achieve those goals, they should be rewarded in the same way that they reward other employees for creating their goals.

Leveraging your architect status for a role in tech
One can of course have a career in technology and architecture in terms of a career path that doesn't focus exclusively on digital technology. There are some good examples of people in the design professions that have risen up, on the technical side, in their organizations to principal or firm owner. Is the career path of somebody focusing on technology clear or is it not clear? According to Fernando Araujo, SCB Associate Principal, Studio Leader and Technical Director:

> The model at SCB takes a little different approach. The model for technical advancement has been a hybrid of the "traditional" roles of a Project Manager and the Technical Architect. Merging these two roles has proven to provide the highest quality and efficiency on a large extent of our work. That said, some projects are of the size and complexity that there is a need for a Senior Technical Architect to share the project's technical responsibility with the Project Manager. In this scenario both people have oversight across multiple projects. Both of these roles are technical career paths. Another path for a technical architect at the Studio level is through the Technical Director role.

Leveraging your talent for technology to manage people
There comes a time in one's career when you have to decide whether remaining hands-on is more important for you than managing, whether people, processes, budgets, and/or schedules. For WeWork's Brian Ringley, there was no equivocating: he wanted to stay involved with technology. He explains:

The way design firms tend to move is a little bit more glacial, a little more step-by-step, and it's a little bit more phased. You might not get a chance to move from researching custom Grasshopper toolsets and interoperable workflows. You might not get to take that next step into, say, programming construction robotics, and construction monitoring drones and things like that. That might not be a step you can take at that practice, because they're not able to roll out a business model that makes sense for that and to support your career. Thus, you may find yourself seeking other firms that are doing something different or feeling out the periphery of the industry or changing industries altogether.

Then there's the other model of just moving from somebody who is interested in being in the trenches and actually doing the technologies, so to speak, like keeping up with programming languages or understanding how to program and control machines, or something like that. There's that mindset where you stay there, but then there's the other mindset, which is "Well, I'm going to do the standard American corporate thing and I'm going to grow in leadership. Then I'm going to build a team, so it's really going to be about managing people. Then I'm a thought leader, and then if I'm lucky enough to be in a firm where you don't have to bring in work to partner, then maybe I can reach partner, but otherwise I'm just a weird special senior role where I'm a thought leader, or maybe I get to be C-level in certain firms and I get to be CTO."

The challenge Ringley set for himself was how to minimize managing people, while keeping his hands on the technology:

I wonder, in this particular era, if we look at the Stevens Institute kids, there are different models we're seeing there, like what Jonatan Schumacher is doing with Konstru is actually pretty fascinating, just looking at that as a model for a career in architecture.

As all of those people start to age and move from being BIM managers, to design technology group leaders, to principals and CTOs, I always start to wonder: is there a saturation point of thought leadership? Probably not. There's probably a healthy appetite out there for consulting and how to manage all this stuff, smart practice and things like that. But for me the challenge is how do I minimize managing people, and how do I always get to keep my hands on the technology? Which is probably naïve. Personally I admire what some of these other people were doing, but I just didn't want to be in a role where I wasn't getting to do the work, and where I was primarily managing people.

There currently are no clear career paths for Superusers. It's make it up as you go, moving from gig to gig, hopefully landing at a place where you're recognized and valued for what you have to offer. "That's a great point about this day and age we're in," offers Stephen Van Dyck, putting a positive spin on Superusers' ambiguous career circumstances. "There's no established understanding of how people with these remarkable skills and abilities should progress as architects." Other Superusers may not see this as positively.

The career risk journey

For whatever reason – to differentiate yourself, to fill a needed role, because you enjoy it, and are good at doing it – you decide to go the route of the design technology specialist. Some see these emerging roles as an exploration, some as a risk – heightened risk, exhilarating, like bungee jumping, only with one's career – but it doesn't deter you from taking this path. You could have plugged yourself into a more

Figure 7.3
Shane Burger
in the Woods
Bagot VR
lounge.
Woods Bagot
developed an
app for iOS
and Android
devices that
allow clients,
using a com-
patible lens,
to walk
through their
designs on
their own
phones.
(2018) Credit:
James and
Karla Murray.

conventional role and title of project designer, project architect, or project manager. Tried and true routes. Familiar routes. Career paths that don't need constant explanation, rationalization, and justification. They will tell you, if you want a 50-year career, be a project manager; if you want a 25-year career, be a project architect; and, if you want to have a 15-year career and roll the dice, be a designer, because it's unlikely every designer becomes a design principal at a firm. They'll just have to, at some point, open their own office, plateau, or count on being the exception. Maybe the titles don't matter to you as much. You're going down this less-trodden path without regrets. You're motivated and energized by it. So, why not take the career path less traveled?

Because the titles for these emerging roles are so ill-defined, the professional trajectory becomes more of a *risk journey* rather than a career path, says Jordan Billingsley:

I would say that the titles are not nearly as important as establishing value and achieving grade levels such as junior associate, associate, senior associate, and so on. There is too much ambiguity in titles whereas corporate hierarchy clearly communicates decision making ability.

One good thing about this type of risk journey is that you at least know that you want to do it, right? It's not something risky where you're not sure how you'll like it. If you start down this path and you feel very stimulated, then you know it's one of those labors of passion. So that's one way to look at it, that's probably how I look at it. It's okay if someone isn't able to see the value of what I'm doing at first. My firm has been very supportive. But in general, if you're doing all these things after hours, it's okay if people don't see the value immediately. Because you're enjoying it, so you'll always have that. Secondly, it'll always make your work easier. Your life will become less stressed, and if you like being the hero in the office, you'll definitely fill that role. You'll become the fireman for a lot of projects. You always get that noble respect from people, or they just say nice things about you more often than they might about a project manager, because you are a problem-fixer. You're not throwing the hammer down on anybody, you are a first responder and everybody respects first responders.

Serving in an emerging role – design technologist, computational designer – is a blue ocean opportunity, one currently with little competition. The "risk journey" seems slightly less risky knowing you can take your specialty on the road and land somewhere safely, giving Superusers some sense of security. Billingsley says:

> It's more of the invisible cap, nobody knows what you go to. Let's say that if you're a computational designer, then you go up to computational BIM, like you're one of those unique people that can do everything and you get to the top, you're not a technology design director and because there's so few of them, your path to design technology director, if that's your ultimate goal, is very narrow and it's going to be more competitive at the top. Everybody has risks, so I wouldn't say it's more risky than the others, but where you end up is less known.

One way to reduce the risk of one's risk journey, is to be exposed to the role on a part-time basis, or reconnaissance. "I believe doing a design technology role part time, is a way of excelling one's career," says Hilda Espinal. "A unique and great opportunity to identify, affect, and articulate the connection between the day-to-day design work and potential of how technology can enhance it and in many cases, further enable it."

Career path cases: part II

There are nearly as many career paths taken by technology trailblazers in the AE profession and industry as there are technology trailblazers. Here, in their own words, are testaments to what can be achieved with talent, hard work, emotionally intelligent handling of circumstances, and opportunities granted.

Design computation leader career path

Dan Anthony, Design Computation Leader, NBBJ:

Stanford is a great place. The skills I had majoring in Management Science and Engineering, an engineering specialty area that comes out of industrial design. By the time I arrived at Stanford, where industrial design was heading was more digital. If you're getting really good at managing complex processes that are interacting, pretty soon you come to realize that has application to software and other spaces beyond machines and a factory. That's where what I was studying was heading. I was interested in this because it combined all of these things that I was passionate about. It combined physical design, computer science, and math, in creation of a process. I enjoyed my major. It basically offered a lot of things to learn for the time while I was there. I appreciated the thoroughness of the broad swath of offerings. But the truth is that one of the things it didn't include was design. Which was a curious omission. From an engineer's standpoint, you can solve a problem. You don't need to explore iterations or options. At the time, Stanford didn't have an architecture school or program. The Stanford d.school wasn't yet the renowned entity it is today. In 2005, it didn't have a real prominent existence. Because I wasn't a graduate student or mechanical engineer, I wasn't exposed to the d.school. Stanford recently founded a school of architecture that comes out of the environmental performance space.

At NBBJ, when people elevate in this role of Design Computation Leader they end up taking in IT, they take in BIM, they take in license management. There is going to be one person at the top. It's similar to design principals: they may be these amazing designers and drawers, but in their new role spend all day orchestrating others. That's part of being elevated. You see their career paths and understand what's expected. I would caution us to avoid looking at history. One truth is that eventually, the nascent or new thing is always bubbling up to challenge the basis of who should lead. As I continue in the profession, I would hope to gather talent underneath me that is doing things I have no idea how to do. I would want them to be: Why, Dan, are we even using Grasshopper over this new machine-learning platform? I don't even have to turn my computer on, just log onto the web and it automatically pages through my Revit model patching up all the missing information. The most important thing is that I understand the value of what that tool or process is, how it's going to be used. It's an inevitability that I can't keep up with everything. But what I can do is understand what it's doing and why it's doing it. When you look at a design practice like ours, or any other type of architectural practice, and look forward to the kind of future we're facing, the leaders and principals of the future are going to face the fact that a lot of these revolutions are things that architects are trying to adapt to. Architecture's funny in that it is slow to change, and there are rules that make us slow to change. The design principal of the future will try to understand technology because it is becoming the water we swim in every day. There are going to be more Shane Burgers – design technologists who rise to the top of organizations, and not in IT or CIO roles but as firm principals and partners. It's also going to specialize a little more. Computation tries to use a technique to take in a lot of things. There may still be somebody who is interested in performance. Somebody who is interested in the human experience. Some people are interested in design techniques – but the techniques they use may also be the automations that help us cycle through various construction methods. Tools and processes that help us to manage construction as a specialty. A role that may look like the current Director of Technology, but it may be the Principal for Construction, who also happens to be using a lot of technology.

I can think of a couple former colleagues who, one, either left to go somewhere where they could be more specialized, or they went somewhere where they can be part of the transformation of a practice. There are certain practices that you can identify where they are trying to catch up on this. Where having someone who is well practiced and part of a team like ours, they can be the seed of new skills to jumpstart this effort in another organization. We pay attention to that, too. The person who hired me is Andrew Heumann who himself has gone through that transformation of architecture, to more specialized architecture, to technology. That's a path, too, that we pay attention to. It's a possibility. The first step isn't necessarily a jump to tech. It's a search for a type of practice that suits your way of thinking. Which practices excel in this space? All practices excel and all practices have problems. What people are seeing is that there is a transformation that's coming that's poorly understood. And we're all trying to understand it. In grad school I ran with a crowd who were trying to be computationally savvy. And are now in practices that are trying to do that. And struggling, because they see that people are appreciating their skills but also doesn't feel like it's fitting in right. When you see people jump from firm to firm they are trying to find an environment where people are coping with this the right way. What you'll find is that some things are working at that firm, and some things aren't. They'll jump to somewhere else and find that OK now we've got a better structure but the projects don't match it. There still is no fundamental solution to that problem.

Principal career path

Stephen Van Dyck, Principal at LMN Architects:

I discovered in grad school that Rhino was the same software that naval architects used. For a while, I thought I wanted to be a boat designer. I really like naval architecture, form following function in the most elemental way. It produces aesthetics, which are the byproduct of the functional requirements. Performance-driven design. And naval architects have been using Rhino for many years. When I learned that the tool that naval architects were using was now a tool that I could use to design buildings, it opened my thinking about how you could design. Boats obviously are really different than buildings, but the tool is so much more nimble and capable of a lot more than AutoCAD or Bentley was capable of.

In my last semester of school design studio with Greg Pasquarelli I became completely immersed in Rhino. We were just explicit modeling. But I got facile enough with it to be able to understand what it could do and do things quickly in it. Then it was my main design tool when I began working at SHoP Architects. Then, simultaneously, a couple friends somehow got a crack copy of CATIA. I had just taken a class in Generative Components over at Stevens Institute. I figured there would be a whole new paradigm in relationship-based modeling. "If: this; then: that." Simultaneously learning generative components and CATIA opened my mind to a completely different design process. You don't have to have an idea, do the work to validate it, find the problems, and then redo all the work again. In fact, in a relationship-based process, it's all flexible. That was really the time when I gained a huge appreciation for new tools. Of course, today, I'm pretty far off the curve of capability with these tools. In fact, I wouldn't ever say that I was an advanced user of any technology. I just happened to know enough to be dangerous. That's actually an important thing I would tell students. Then, you've got to say, "Okay, who else has this knowledge out there that I can collaborate with?" And if you don't have these tools in hand, or

Figure 7.4
Stephen Van
Dyck leading
a design
meeting
during the
design phase
for the
Voxman
School of
Music. (2018)
Credit: LMN
Architects.

people in the office with the corresponding skillset, maybe you need to make investments. Attract and educate for new skills to enable the implementation of new ways of working. I wouldn't say my story is one of a design technologist so to speak. It's a bit more general and happens to include technology.

My time with Robert Venturi, Denise Scott Brown, and Steven Izenour was hugely influential for me because when I started working for them I was a student of architectural history, not architecture. I understood why their ideas mattered in a broader context of the narratives of architectural history. Working with them implicitly taught me the concept of relevance at the historical level, which has always been important to me. That's an anecdote of how mentoring has affected me. Phil Bernstein has always agitated my thinking in good ways. He has pushed me to address the professional existential question, always harping on [about] realities of current practice and all the constraints we live within. We have contracts. We've got delivery model problems. We've got technology hurdles. All of these things go into the problem of being an architect. Gregg Pasquarelli has been, and continues to be, an important mentor to me. He is constantly questioning the traditional approach to architecture. He has no misgivings, or no preconception, of mixing business, economic performance, concerns of stakeholders into his model of the profession. That is fundamental to him, that we must approach our profession from a broad perspective that thrives on new and often shunned inputs. The diversity of perspective that we bring to bear as thinkers is critical. It's at the core our value proposition.

Partner career path

Matthew Krissel, Partner at KieranTimberlake:

I started as a summer intern and have touched every role in this office. One thing that has served me well is that I have been an active designer of my own relationship to people and technology. It helped me extend my potential and I wasn't going to let new responsibilities prevent me from growing in this area. It does require more work and it does require the mindset and genuine interest, but I don't agree that people can't evolve in a way that

Figure 7.5
To sustain an ethos of innovation in its rapidly growing architecture firm, Kieran-Timberlake envisioned a platform for all individuals to extend knowledge, creativity, and innovation across projects. The firm redesigned relationships between disciplines to encourage knowledge flow, new connections, and freedom to experiment. (2018) Credit: KieranTimberlake.

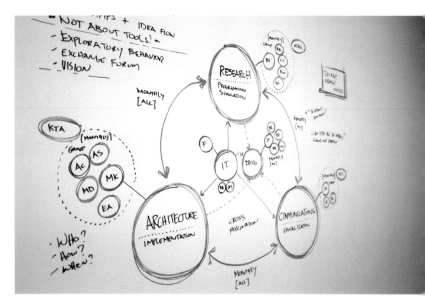

still meets all the other demands of leadership. Instead of avoiding the tools, it means I now use them a little differently than others, and I set out to make that difference something that can still contribute to the work. It is incredible to think of how far I have come and where I am now. Like many, I have benefited from other people's generosity with their time and support along the way, but you do also have to be an advocate for yourself. I was fortunate to learn a long time ago the value of who we chose to surround ourselves with and the impact those decisions have on our lives. Regardless of where you go to school, your beginnings, or inherent advantages, being around smart and talented people motivates and pushes oneself to make the best of whatever situation you're in.

I also was fortunate with my timing and that I worked for several years after college instead of going straight through to graduate school. That meant I attended graduate school from 2003–2005, right at the peak of the transition towards the digital. It was a special time in our field's collective history, and one that I am grateful to have participated in while in school. Seeing design and design methods shift so dramatically away from the analog was critical for me, especially since I had the advantage of being educated on both sides of this history of architecture. Learning

design and making by hand as well as through advanced computa-
tion and digital fabrication allowed me to discover my own voice
within the design world. While I have come a long way, it still feels
like it is just the beginning.

The late Gen X and early Gen Y designers who trained and
practiced on both sides of the analog and digital tool set are in a
great position to lead the profession forward on balancing the two.
It is important to acknowledge the confluence of other changes
that coincided in the mid-2000s. Software and hardware are
obvious, but more important is the cultural change of sharing
coupled with new business models and platforms for design. This
evolution, with access to cheap memory and speed, was an
accelerant for a design environment with significantly fewer bar-
riers to computation, networking knowledge, and exploration in
architecture firms. For me, working on both sides of this offered
clarity to the incredible opportunity here. It is also important to
remember that this speed and access caused many to not learn
some key foundational elements about designing parameters, prin-
ciples, and the mindset around these emerging workflows which
are critical skills that too often have been lost. Learning to build a
perspective by hand is incredibly valuable to working in the com-
puter. This is the same in photography and the continued value in
experimenting with film. The foundations of composition, how the
human eye works, understanding dynamic range are confronted in
analog workflows, but software and hardware have unintentionally
subverted much of this meaning. This often results in a laissez-
faire approach where one will just fix it all in post-production. The
need to be aware, conscious, and clear on early decisions impact-
ing modeling, simulation, and visualization downstream are heigh-
tened when it is labor intensive to change variables. So, it required
great intentionality and purpose in the analog-only era. Being in
command of the fundamentals and involved in the design of the
early parameters are critical skills for computationally driven prac-
tices that seek to do meaningful work. To be clear, I'm not
interested in going back to that "slow space," but there is no
doubt that parts of working manually are a great precursor and
learning tool for working digitally. I would rather we enhance our
education to evolve and bring those valuable principles and meth-
odologies forward into a digital workflow.

The next generation of you

"Ironically, like computers, we have to find a common language between the sources," says Cameron. He elaborates:

Communication often breaks down when a traditional architect doesn't understand when a technologist creates the model with a short script. What you find is that it's not about drawings any- more, which a lot of traditional architects resist. At this point in history, it creates a conflict between the conventional and uncon- ventional groups – as you might imagine. Instead, prove the problem-solving skills, time savings, and accuracy that computa- tion can bring. As for a career path, to some degree this is a new venture in architecture and a lot of us have had to forge that in our own way. One dictum holds true: In order to lead, you need followers. Only a portion of your career advancement is technical knowledge. You must lead and communicate with people.

Leaders are always looking for people who will one day replace them – it's part of the territory of being a firm leader. Shane Burger says:

The best conversations I've had within Woods Bagot have been around not so much I *need a Grasshopper person*, or I need someone to do this in Revit. Or we need to make this funky façade look right in the rendering. The better conversations are ones when that non-design technologist realizes that the person I'm talking to represents the future of my position. You are the next generation of me.

Design technologists who also design, or who become full-time designers, is a more complex topic that deserves a chapter of its own, and will be covered next.

Note

1 *DesignIntelligence Quarterly*, 3Q, 2017 p.103.

Chapter 8

Design technologists as digitally savvy designers

Design and technology: a false dichotomy from the start, by the artificially siloed college curricula, then perpetuated into the profession. Additionally, technology has been misused in the formal obsession with computational pavilions, twisty buildings, and other structures requiring complex geometry for its own sake, and a too-narrow and sterile a definition of optimization. Design technologists return technology to design, figuring out how to incorporate both analog and digital technology into projects, team workflows, and their firms' work processes – not for its own sake but to improve the design, functionality, livability, and affordability of projects. Design technologists look for opportunities for technology to make them better designers – and their designs better: earlier defined, more rapidly iterated, higher-quality design.

In the previous chapter, we looked at design technologists as architects and managers. Here, in this chapter, we focus on design technologists who are, or who aspire or are urged by their firms to become, designers. Designers who are computationally savvy, influencing the design process – and building designs – through computational means. Design technologists who also design, or who become full-time designers, leveraging their talent for technology on building design projects. Design technologists who have an interest in being a designer, whether technology serves as an impediment, or expediter to their becoming designers. The chapter asks whether designers, technical project architects, or managers represent the future of design technologists, and concludes with a look at *the third space*, where design technologists are proactively designing the design process.

Design: data-driven, generative, and predictive

Let's start by defining what we mean by *design*, because the way we design is changing. Yes, designing in a Moleskine or on trace for some is still de rigueur. For others, designing has changed due to the introduction of new computational tools that leverage data, algorithms, and the cloud. But the technology is not what's driving this change: it's risk.

On project teams, architects and engineers take a design from a state of uncertainty and ambiguity to one of clarity and certainty. Architects may be comfortable with ambiguity, but owners require certainty. To address this need for certainty, many activities designers undertake today are being transformed into data, and many tasks of the design process are being automated. So, with predictive design tools one designs – like Autofill – anticipating our next move. With generative design one designs leveraging algorithms and parametric modeling within predetermined constraints. And, with data-driven design one designs by manipulating data, not form.[1]

Data-driven design is more straightforward than it sounds. "I think of attacking the most-asked questions in design," says DLR Group's Ryan Cameron. He continues:

> For starters, am I meeting my program area requirements? We are always improving the process of extracting that information from the common data environment. At different stages of the project we extract the room information, review what has changed, and what is meeting the criteria. The client requests program data, and we compare it to the model data to help inform the design. Is it within an acceptable percentage? If true, proceed. If false, make corrections. It's pretty simple. Design has a lot of gray areas and creating a process that eliminates gray from black and white has yielded better results.[2] Outside the "bubble," this is a revolutionary way to design.
>
> Some might argue it's just an evolution of the practice, but to systematically have an understanding of computer code to augment design processes takes a different person. Hand drafting went to CAD and some say to BIM. Now to connected BIM? That would be a natural curve. However, assimilating research to a common data environment that is augmented by AI to create a design is very different than dreaming something up and modeling

what you want. In less than 20 years I predict we won't be modeling in the traditional sense anymore.

Today a growing vocal minority – the *Superusers* of this book – speak of scripts and algorithms as integral to their design process. They use visual programming tools to automate and complete work in hours that might otherwise take days. They create cloud-enabled data visualizations as a real-time by-product of the design act, where data not only informs their intuition but improves it. They design with adaptive parametric smart elements that use rules to govern what the user can do, so when something moves or changes everything moves or changes with it. Indeed, much of our design has already been outsourced – not overseas, or even to people, but – to software.[3] "The challenges that face BIM Coordinators and Design Technology leaders are incredibly stimulating," says Jordan Billingsley. He continues:

> As students we barely scratch the surface of the technologies that we interact with daily and my eyes are just beginning to open to the data-driven possibilities – including design. While I am not looking to segue back into being a building designer, I do see a path of influencing the design process through computational means.

Design and technology

Design in school often becomes stigmatized, the be-all and end-all for architecture students. In the courses I teach, I don't distinguish between design and technology. I treat the two as equals, where technology is integral to design, and vice versa. Firms also have to wrestle with the fact that seemingly every recent gradate wants to design and be a designer. It's a relief when a graduate voluntarily says they would like to be a project architect or work on the technical side of projects. SCB's Fernando Araujo says:

> When a young person is brought into our firm, the name of the position provided to them is Designer Technical. That reinforces the way we're looking at it, that everything is designed, whether you're designing the massing of the building or doing the core layout, you are designing. And we have to look at the design from all the different aspects, not just the aesthetic but also the

technical portion of it, because at the end of the day we're not just doing Photoshop renderings. We want to realize our buildings. We're a full service architectural firm that wants to have our work built.

As WeWork Senior Researcher Brian Ringley tweeted:

Can we please stop the false dichotomy of design and technology? The false dichotomy of design and technology severely limits career paths and reflects poorly on firm's integration of technology. Gee why are all the talented people leaving architecture? If BIM manager and project manager isn't the same role at your office, then ... bye bye.[4]

One firm where design and technology are integrated is CannonDesign. "All the guys and gals in it are really good with technology," says Hilda Espinal. She continues:

It's leader and lead designer, Mehrdad Yazdani, gets it. He builds teams of talented designers embracing of technology. Not only do they have the talent and ability to push boundaries, they also have the resources and time to experiment and innovate. It is their normal process, generating award-winning designs. I'm grateful this isn't an isolated case. Much of our office leadership, our Design Director, David Polzin and all the way to our CEO, Brad Lukanic, encourage it. I realize this isn't the case everywhere or even universally at my firm, but if it is entirely up to me to select the staff for my design studio, I will hands down want people that are comfortable with technology, those who master (it) and to whom it is second nature. They do have to be whole architects though, it is a crucial part of the skillset in our DNA, just not all of it ...

I always try to emphasize that one of my main goals for our firm and our industry is to help people understand that Design and Technology can very successfully augment each other and, they're not mutually exclusive.

It is, thankfully, a very different and easier proposition then back when I decided to pursue a path at the intersection of both. For me then, over 15 years ago, it came down to some tough question such as "Should I leave architecture to do this?" "How, exactly, will I do it?" "What if it isn't what I envision, will I be able to go back to project work or will I be setting myself behind my peers?" Thankfully my boss then at Lohan Associates allowed me to give it a whirl, and assured me that if I wanted to go back to project work, he'd likely have multiple opportunities for me to jump into as Project Architect. That was incredibly helpful and it just boiled down to "How DO you do it?" And so, my answer revealed itself as I focused on how the two came together, and not what separated them. This became looking at the potential with lenses of technology-augmented-architecture. Later I realized how this dynamic could be bidirectional. So, my advice is to start to analytically look at how you can find opportunities in your designs and projects to leverage available technology or shape technology in ways that meet your specific needs, ideas, aspirations, and use cases.

Technology enables design

It can be an incredibly empowering moment when one discovers how they can leverage technology to realize their designs. "One of the key problems that I found when in school was that for every project that we did in studio, we had to submit a physical model," explains Ana Garcia Puyol. She continues:

I had this phrase in my head, from one of my teachers, "You can only build what you know how to draw." And to me, the opposite problem was true. Like in architecture school, in the professional world, I could only design that that I could build in a model. I felt incredibly limited by the technology that I had at home in Spain, and then suddenly I came here to the US, and I saw that these machines, new technology, was available to me, so then I could go ahead and design many things that I had imagined that I could not make possible in the past. Back then, with virtual models, I was OK, but I definitely couldn't make walls with a doubly curved surface because I didn't have the means to fabricate them. That was incredibly frustrating for me because I'm attracted to complexity in design.

Design technologist as non-designer

Some design technologists are decidedly designers, while others play a consulting role in service to design. Since the late 2000s

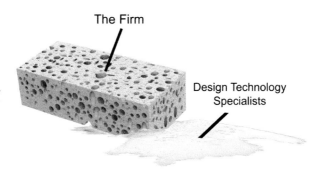

The Firm

Design Technology
Specialists

there has been a succession of technology-related roles in architecture and engineering firms: CAD manager, BIM manager, Computational BIM Manager, and so on. Where is this heading? To the next role-of-the-day? Or where these roles are absorbed into pre-existing positions within the firm? WeWork Senior Researcher, Brian Ringley says:

The mindset of the design technologist is "I'm going to integrate these new technologies into standard practice to elevate practitioners so that the definition of practice is dynamic."

More and more, technology is assumed to be part of standard practice, but the design technologists themselves probably have little interest in being a designer. It's impossible to speak for everyone. There are lots of different motivations out there, but at least from what I've seen from my small esoteric circle, is we have an interest in enhancing or continually redefining what it means to be a designer relative to technology. But we ourselves are not interested in being designers per se. Then that always just begs the question of "What is my career?" You could have a dynamic career as an architectural researcher, as another way of saying design technologist, of just constantly being curious and finding new technologies and incorporating them into practice. That's possible.

Yet, when I'm teaching, that's by and large what everyone wants to be, with few exceptions. This semester I'm teaching a seminar that's specifically about the technical delivery of façades and what the data workflow is for that. Because it was an elective, you actually get those students who are like, "I really want to understand how this works, but usually it's this uphill battle." It's like, "Well, I came here to be famous and to work completely by myself, and to be beholden only to my own genius." That's just something that we've never really done a good job of, to stop perpetuating those myths.

People really think designing is super-sacred and is like something apart from technology. It's all a little silly. It stunts the careers of really promising young designers, because from day one they're taught the value – being a designer over being a technologist – and I have personally experienced working with designers who were really promising with the technology, who actually just wanted to walk away from the technology because of their concern that they would no longer be a designer or an architect. The other thought that arises is with an example of Nate Miller, which is: we can design, too. It's not sacred, it's not magic. We also went to architecture school. I can make beautiful things and that has a set of values unto itself. I just never really consciously made the distinction. The distinction I did make is, "If I become a designer I'll never get paid commensurate to my value and I'll be worked to death." The distinction I made was out of the culture of being a designer is actually pretty toxic, so I will market myself as somebody who's more into technology so that I have a better life.

Design technologist as digitally savvy designer

One finding from my conversations with design technologists is that former design technologists and computational design leaders today

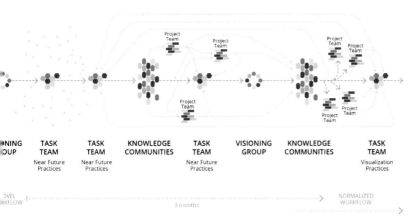

Figure 8.2 KieranTimberlake's digital design platform includes teams with distinct interests and functions. The Visioning Group, Task Teams, and Knowledge Communities work together to create a framework for exploring, experimenting, and quickly normalizing innovative workflows among architectural teams. (2018) Credit: KieranTimberlake.

consider themselves simply designers. What's behind this trend? Too much work and someone has to do it? A swing away from process to product? Design technology was just a way to differentiate yourself early on, whereas everybody secretly really just wants to design anyway.

"There are a lot of ill-defined titles for new emerging roles in the field of architecture that are based on vestiges of AutoCAD terminology and expectations," explains Jordan Billingsley. He continues:

> Nevertheless, I do see a logical splintering of traditional roles into partially fulfilling these new roles: Designers will remain as the most likely pool of candidates to draw from to develop "Computational Designers," "Project Architects" (if given the resources to develop programming skills) would be well suited for "Computational BIM" roles, and a very small portion of Project Managers would be capable of transitioning to a Design Technology Director position. Each of these traditional positions has historical strengths that can transition to Design Technology roles if they are provided an environment that fosters a computational mindset.

"One thing I would like to do more of is to organize a little more strategic thinking on how we're going to make the techniques we have be useful for everyone," says Dan Anthony. He continues:

> Part of that requires staying cognizant of what the design problems are. But also producing or making more, in a digital sense. Part of that is I want people to continue to populate the role of the digitally savvy designer. In order to do that, we need to keep feeding them the better method.

As founding member and former leader of LMNts, LMN's Scott Crawford was once squarely in the tech space. Now, in addition to firm Principal, he is considered a full-time project designer. Does his background in tech, where working in complex parametric modeling systems has become his design process, enable him to approach projects differently? "It definitely does," says Crawford:

> I'm now more than ever in a position to set up opportunities on projects that previously I might not have been aware of given my

more focused involvement. This greater awareness of what is happening overall has been helpful for finding new means of collaborating or recognizing areas that a new technology might be implemented. Whether that be a new piece of software or innovative material system.

How a firm bridges design and technology: a case

As a research-based practice with an interest in creating knowledge, KieranTimberlake takes a comprehensive approach to design, one where technology is only one component. Says partner Matthew Krissel:

The design technologist skillset is only one facet of a designer and it is not the only thing that defines the role. That's been true whether it was a person more skilled in hand-drawing or now with a person more adept at using a computer. Well-formed teams and organizations should have a varied set of skills, experiences, and expertise. The more important question is how well they work together because of their differences.

Everyone here is a designer, researcher, and creator of knowledge through continuous learning. We are all as committed to sharing ideas as we are to creating them. Research, asking questions, and restless curiosity are part of our culture.

KieranTimberlake is always looking at the breadth of what they're doing, where they have been, and where they want to go. We have learned that digital initiatives must go beyond stewardship and software training. You must build discourse, create collective fluency, and have formal and informal ways for people to explore, build, and share ideas. In 2013 we stepped back and reframed the question we were asking about digital design.

We asked, "How might digital design expand our creative potential, discover new opportunities, and amplify our ability to deliver exemplary projects?" This led to KieranTimberlake's Digital Design Mission Statement, which became: *Improve how we create knowledge, iterate ideas, synthesize information, design, build and communicate our work.* This is how KieranTimberlake does it: by asking who, why, what, and how; by identifying salient firm characteristics, defining terms, and setting expectations.

This framework goes beyond one or two people managing standards. This is about everybody in the firm having skin in the game as a true community of designers. Everybody shares these collective goals.

Who
The digital design platform is the combination of people, processes, and technology. All design staff are given time and resources to engage in exploratory behavior, knowledge sharing, idea discovery, and implementation for individual and collective development and growth.

Why
Designers have a unique ability and obligation to take on the great challenges of our time. We want to explore ideas outside of the limitations of projects, ask smarter questions and create a more informed environment for design. Data coupled with intuition, combinatorial thinking, and digital tools helps us see, retain, communicate, and synthesize more.

Extending our minds in this way allows us to connect knowledge in ways that were invisible before. We begin to see new connections between disparate ideas and generate new insight into problems.

Architects need to drive emergent computation and technology systems to design and deliver meaningful work that elevates the human experience.

What
Build discourse and guide initiatives that scrutinize the architecture industry, anticipate and identify emerging needs and adjacent opportunities, and set near and long-term aspirations for our practice.

Through collective intelligence, inquiry and vision foster inclusive forums and task teams that drive our capability to evolve with and speculate on technological advancements that elevate the design and construction of our work.

How
With a digital landscape that is perpetually evolving and essential, we recognize there is no destination but rather a persistent state

of becoming. We must effectively practice, engage, and thrive within the knowledge structures of data, information, and virtual/physical experiences to continuously expand our design potential.

Cultivate a trans-disciplinary environment and mindset that supports curiosity, unconventional thinking, and collective fluency.

Promote the value of experimentation and the virtue of failing forward. Ensure that time, flexibility, and resources to explore ideas, tools, and workflows is available to everyone.

Continue to develop new and creative ways to work in an open marketplace of ideas throughout the digital design platform.

Characteristics

Digital practices are pervasive. It's critical that they are present in every aspect of the firm, and in our projects as testbeds. It's important that we work out new ideas on real projects with real deadlines and pressures, not only with idealized conditions.

We are data-nimble and tool agnostic as we exploit new capabilities that technology can provide. We work collectively, asking questions, and combining ideas. We seek new problems to solve, and consciously put ourselves in unfamiliar territories so we can search for answers.

Computation is more than the multiplication of ideas, it is essential to the possibility of ideas. We are clear on vision and loose on details. We distribute agency, remain open to change, and course correct along the way. One constant is that technology is always changing. You must see digital design as constantly emerging, without fixed or attainable stasis points. We avoid being too precise about tactics and details to remain nimble.

One of the mistakes I have observed other firms make in the context of digital design, BIM and digital tools, is conflation of aspirations and goals. The drive to make the process better, easier, and more efficient is an important aspiration, something we should work on, but it is not the goal. Making great projects is the goal and often the path there is not always efficient. However, because digital design or computational tools are often associated with productivity and efficiency, people will gravitate towards tasks and not goals. Too often the people using them are focused on the pressing issues of a project and are not thoughtfully organized and operating around a strategic, goal-driven vision. The expedient cannot be driving the organization.

It is important to have the vision and goals in place with great clarity and agreement and a leadership core that understands these differences. This, along with a healthy mix of goal-driven and task-driven people allows an organization to really execute and deliver great work where computational design is a natural part of our thinking and making. This expands our creative potential, catalyzes imagination, drives meaningful exploration, and creates new possibilities in the built environment.

How does KieranTimberlake accomplish this? Krissel says:

What we've found is that it can't be top down or bottom up, it has to be both. Some ideas are tangential and come when reflecting on the practice from a distance. Others come because of a very specific project situation or emerge from the dynamics of a group. We've developed a knowledge network and idea flow for multiple streams to be harvested, to converge and shape our practice for the better. We have a Digital Design Visioning Group that meets quarterly to set a clear and broad vision for firm-wide digital practices. Key staff help build out the vision, generate momentum, and execute the tactics. We see the flow of ideas across our practice as generating a larger perspective and range for the whole organization. We augment this with weekly task teams comprised of a range of people from across the firm who share knowledge and tackle immediate issues together. We also hold Tools and Workflows sessions at every project phase, where we sync the whole team with people on other projects to connect the latest practices and workflows office wide. These meetings provide space for designers to speculate on what tools they will need and what practices they will want to deploy on their projects in real time. We talk about what questions the team is going to be asking, and how they will answer them. Do we already own that tool? Do we have to make it?

Firms absorbing technologists

Earlier, we discussed how the design technology specialist is seen as "the Other," how there is a stigma attached to the role, one of a

rracotta Façade – Attractor to Generate the Global Pattern of Openness

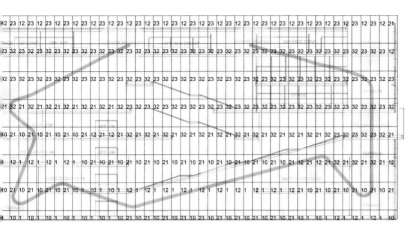

Figure 8.3
Diagram of
south façade
for the Health
Sciences
Innovation
Building at
University of
Arizona
showing
pathway
regions of
façade open-
ness with
overload
panel type
numbers
indicated.
(2018) Credit:
CO
Architects.

consultant or perpetual outsider to the mainstream work of the office: namely, *design*. "As more designers at all levels of organizations effectively using computation, I would like to see it so pervasive that the novelty of it being something unique disappears," says Matthew Krissel. He continues:

Just expect it as part of the way that we work as designers. Just like no one asks you if you're good at email anymore, I look forward to getting beyond the fixation of these differences that I believe are a distraction to the design community. People can get so preoccupied by the polish or glare from technology that we have missed the fact that many have been spending all this time and energy using this opportunity on superfluous things. Using computation to create solutions looking for problems is backwards and unproductive.

The obsolescence of design technology specialists

Do design technology specialists have built-in obsolescence, the way much of the tech they use does? In being absorbed by the firm in a lead design role, does LMN's Scott Crawford represent the future of design technologists? "Traditionally, we've referred to our Tech Studio members as design technologists," says principal Stephen

Van Dyck. "Part of the problem with this is it inherently separates the role from the act of design. With the term design technologist you're saying that it's not part of the core design pursuit."

Some firms start a tech studio, and they do it primarily for marketing reasons. LMNts seems to be thoroughly integrated – so much so, it's getting harder to distinguish it as a separate entity. Is LMN's Tech Studio a part of the culture of LMN Architects? "Unquestionably," says Van Dyck. "The products of Tech Studio, as built in real projects, have demonstrated the power of integrating technology our design and delivery process." Van Dyck continues:

Taking that further, I had this idea originally when we were creating Tech Studio, that the ideal scenario would be if the group made itself obsolete. That everything that the group does, and the things that they can develop, the methods of working, and the idea of being in a constant state of inquiry into how we can improve ourselves, would become essential to how we all operate.

Broadly speaking, I think that is beginning to happen. The group has developed tools and ways of working which have become more standard to how we operate. The culture of inquiry and research is spreading. It's a great win.

With the more widespread adoption of these ways of working in the office, and the simultaneous kind of slowing of overall change in the specific to software, LMN's Tech Studio has shifted its focus in the last few years in two ways. Says Van Dyck:

One, we've begun to deploy some of these experts on projects full-time. Because ultimately, these skills for working with tools, and this idea of becoming obsolete, contributes to making this how everybody operates. Every team, every project, every architect and designer should have these skills. Why not put your money where your mouth is and actually have those people become the designers?

The other aspect is we've explored more and more this territory of interactive technologies. We haven't done much writing or publishing about any of this stuff yet. But been spending a lot of time with both sensing technology and human-computer interaction, and particularly some hardware and software design that allows responsive systems to be enabled.

"LMNts' shift in focus was in response to a number of influences," says Scott Crawford. He continues:

Early on, we tried to do a lot of in-house staff training in order to spread computational skills widely throughout the office. That proved more difficult than we expected because of the constant project deadlines and our underestimating of how much time it actually took for people to learn and then adopt these tools into their workflow. Another factor was that early on a lot of the things we were focusing on were low hanging fruit like inter-operability. While those challenges haven't completely disap-peared, there are a lot more start-ups and open source projects that are focusing solely on that. Now we've shifted our focus to exploring how we can expand our design capabilities and also dig into some more significant research that have the potential to carve out new design space for architects.

Questions arise from this predicament: Will a new tech studio be required when new technologies (e.g. AI) are introduced into the practice? And in this scenario, when the tech studio is absorbed, what becomes of design technology specialists who have dedicated their careers to a technology role? If they're lucky, they become Scott Crawford. "I would argue that contemporary software improvements, unlike the easy early wins we had several years ago, are probably going to require larger groups of software specialists, which generally, a design firm like ours can't afford," says Van Dyck. "A good example of that is TT's CORE Studio, which is I believe 19 people now. They have real horsepower and are developing some amazing things." As discussed previously, TT CORE Studio, once 100% overhead, has become 50/50 billable, and has spun-off tools like Konstru.

How did it come about and what does it mean for the future, that one of the founding members of LMN's Tech Studio didn't remain a design technologist, and is now a full-time project designer? "Scott's most direct path to becoming a design leader was his ability to design in complex parametric modeling systems," says Van Dyck. "That's just become his design process, and part of that is making."

Scott Crawford also built LMN's first CNC mill in his garage. "He got a low-interest credit card, and then my friend Jack and I joined him, and we made a little company called Frankenstein to allow Scott to write off his garage!" explains Van Dyck. He continues:

After building a bunch of personal projects we began building mockups of the stuff we were designing at the office, to learn and prove that they could be made. It was a very grassroots thing. Scott is like a maker and a tinkerer, and a designer, really, at heart. It's clear to me that someone with those skills, talents, and interests should be leading the design of buildings, not simply working as a design technologist.

Most firm's tech studios are in support of core pursuits, including design. Van Dyck says:

It's a lens that we're going to look at this through. It's like sustainability. You can't just say, "Oh, we're going to put the sustainability team on this and make it better." That never ends well. These motives must come from the core. The leadership of the project must establish it as a priority for the process, in collaboration with the builder and the client.

These days we are finding that some of our members of Tech Studio – our technologists – are evolving to become leading designers and practitioners. As a design leader, you're no longer the person in the corner who keeps advocating for interoperability, fixing someone's Grasshopper definition, or trying to implement simulation in the working process. The best technologists should be making decisions, integrating technology thorough design and delivery, not acting as consultants. So, until we have those people – the technologists who become design leaders – in design leadership, in direct contact with the owner, helping to plan out the project's schedule and staffing approach, technology is always going to be sidelined. To me, that's where the big shift will come. In the next five or so years we're going to see that there will be more people with the so-called technologist backgrounds leading design teams, and then we won't be having this conversation.

Figure 8.4
The University of Arizona Health Sciences Innovation Building terracotta and glass rainscreen under construction. (2018) Credit: CO Architects.

Computational designer/designer career path cases

What follows are examples of career paths taken by trailblazers in the AE profession and industry who have leveraged technology in their work as designers. Here, in their own words, are examples of what they have achieved with their talent, hard work, handling of their circumstances, and the opportunities they were granted.

Designer career path

Scott Crawford, Principal, LMN Architects:

I've always considered myself to be a designer first. Prior to working for LMN, I worked for a few one-man residential architecture practices and a public artist so I definitely had some experience to gain around how to apply my skills to this new scale of practice. Initially, taking on the role of design technologist allowed me to help out on a wide variety of somewhat isolated building systems; facades, screens, daylight analysis, etc. This helped me to get a feel for how things were done, but over time I found that the type of design problems people were asking for help with weren't changing.

167

Figure 8.5
The Univer-
sity of Ari-
zona Health
Sciences
Innovation
Building
panels are
modeled
after the ribs
of the
saguaro
cactus, which
is native to
the local
Sonaran
Desert. (2018)
Credit: CO
Architects.

Essentially, the role of computation in design was being determined by those not using it. That caused me to reach out to the LMN leadership and continually ask for higher levels of design responsibility. It was my belief that it was as important to design the process as the product that resulted from it and to do this I needed to be part of the effort to define the design problem.

A positive benefit that I saw from working as design technologist was the autonomy that I sometimes received. I was seen as having a certain expertise that allowed me to help guide the direction of a project even though my number of years of experience might be significantly less than someone I was working under.

I've struggled with the title of design technologist at times during my career. Sometimes the labels we choose to give things can unfortunately narrow our understanding. There's been a tendency I've noticed for people to assume that what I do is push a magical combination of buttons on the computer and then the computer manages to generate a solution for me. From my perspective that couldn't be further from the truth, but it did limit for a while how people thought I should be engaged on projects. Over time, it's become apparent to others that it's not just a matter of teaching people how the hardware or software operates, but that there is a mindset or design approach that is also necessary in engaging these tools. I've had to demonstrate this to others in the office and even our collaborators on projects, and that in the end people's eyes have been opened up to the fact that computation brings a set of design possibilities to the profession that were not available before.

When we started LMNts, one of the intentions was for us to find new tools to bring into the office. I had learned how to use a 3-Axis CNC machine while I was at the University of Washington and was excited to continue experimenting with that tool. I went to the leadership of LMN sometime in 2011 or so and asked if I could put together a small shop in the office with the focus being a CNC machine. A proposal was put together, and there was definitely interest from the partners but in the end the concerns about safety, space, and accessibility overweighed their desire to have access to these tools. The situation made sense to me at the time because they were being sold on a tool that seemed cool but there was no practical knowledge to compel them to take the leap. So in early 2012 I did. I started looking around for inexpensive kits that I could purchase and assemble myself and ended up discovering a company called CNC Router Parts that were located only an hour outside Seattle. I mentioned this to my friends/coworkers Stephen and Jack, they said they were in so I got an 18 month 0% APR credit card, purchased the machine, and we were off making dust. We all wanted to use the machine for personal projects, but were also looking for opportunities for how we could prove its use within the office as well as make some money. LMN agreed to pay us for machine time if we used the CNC on LMN projects and within 12 months we had paid off the credit card and had begun to convince the partners that this was something the office should have. The most significant project we built on my machine was The Octahedron, a small pavilion for the 2013 Seattle Design festival, which contained close to 3000 individual pieces held together with only friction. It ended up winning a Seattle AIA Honor Award that year and after that we started to seriously discuss how to set up a shop at LMN. That shop has now been running for a few years, and we been able to get a lot of people in the office to understand how to program a CNC, and expand the maker culture in our office. This fall we'll be building a roughly 2000 square foot acoustic ceiling, containing over 700 unique parts, for a project that I worked on with the Seattle Symphony. We've come a long way in that short time. Things just needed to be proven out to get there.

Design computation leader career path

Hiram Rodriguez, Computational Design Group Leader, Thornton Tomasetti:

A designer has different connotations here at TT. You can be designing a curved façade system, or you can be rationalizing a complex long span system for a stadium, so in theory you are solving a problem through computation methods. However, the process of sketching and conceptualizing those ideas through sketching can vary depending on the problem itself. I do tend to do some hand sketching when the problem becomes too complex. It allows me to step back and think about how to approach the problem at hand. One of the things that I remember the most as an architecture student was that it was easier sometimes to visualize a problem in 2D as a section, get a better understanding of proportion, because at the end of the day we have a building to deliver. Sometimes it's strange because you're working with a range of problems and a range of ages in a group. Therefore, it is hard for people to conceptualize it or visualize it in 3D, and sometimes it is easier to just get a pen and paper, and sketch something very simply. Different age groups will approach the problem differently. I get very excited about seeing some of the stuff that's happening in other industries, or in general software development. Or new ideas and paradigms, and start to think about how they could apply to the built environment, either from a process perspective – the ways we design and build – or product perspective. So they experience this space.

Notes

1 A version of this definition of design originally appeared in Deutsch, Randy, *DesignIntelligence Quarterly*, 2Q, 2018 pp.19–21.
2 Cameron has a program area assessment tool at www.architectma chines.com/library that everyone can use.
3 Deutsch, *DesignIntelligence*.
4 Twitter, October 28, 2017.

Chapter 9

Leading Superusers

When design technology specialists become design technology leaders, there's an understandable shift in priorities and responsibilities. This chapter looks at what design technology leaders do, what it takes to lead and support Superusers, and the need to identify what is advancing in our space that we're not seeing, staying relevant, and the regular need for skill rebuild. Next it looks at what it takes to create an environment that fosters a computational mindset from one's team. The chapter closes with marketing a firm's use of technology, and winning projects by emphasizing technology and the Superusers who create and use it.

CannonDesign's Chief Technology Officer (CTO) Hilda Espinal trusts her teams to take care of familiar headaches and pain points, such as connecting digital tools, and bridging workflow gaps. As a firm leader, she no longer has to do these things herself. The emphasis changes when you rise within an organization, where you find yourself less hands-on, less tactical, and sometimes more strategic – and frequently less billable. Espinal used to think about more tactical things a lot, now less so, in part due to trust, but also due to technology itself, to having access to resources, and in part due to firm culture. As Espinal explains:

> I do, but also part of the reason for this concern decreasing significantly has to do with where I am at now. At CannonDesign we have an environment that's fully virtualized. In all other previous firms, I had to worry about which office is going to collaborate with which one, and what we need to do behind the scenes, IT, a private tunnel or site-to-site connection. Here, I don't. Geographically distributed teams are not an issue. There is no additional preparation or work required to work with someone

Figure 9.1
The award winning Passerelle, both a key bridge and piece of art for the Centre hospitalier de l'Université de Montréal (CHUM) in Montreal. (2018) Credit: CannonDesign + NEUF Architect(e)s.

across my office or overseas. So, I'll just park my laptop where I'm at, including home or a coffee shop, and I'll join the team. Those headaches have gone away for me.

One of the challenges I've always had is funding ideas, things we want to pursue and are non-existent. Especially when these things one envisions do not have hard ROI because it hasn't been done before. And it's more about, not how much time am I going to save or how much more efficient I'm going to be, it's more about what am I going to do that my competitor cannot do? Or I may be able to leverage other benefits that we just don't have metrics for, per se. It's about innovation and creating opportunities.

What design technology leaders do

While weighing the value in improving his own coding abilities, as a Design Computation Leader, NBBJ's Dan Anthony has his team's – and firm's – best interests in mind by looking out for and identifying better ways to get work done. Anthony realizes that he may not get any better or faster at coding. And in the last chapter we saw how he would like to do more strategic thinking on how to make techniques useful for everyone. He recognizes that part of that requires staying cognizant of what the design problems are, but

Figure 9.2
**The award
winning Pas-
serelle, both
a key bridge
and piece of
art CHUM –
Largest
Healthcare
Project in
North Amer-
ica. (2018)
Credit: Can-
nonDesign +
NEUF Archi-
tect(e)s.**

Figure 9.2 The award winning Passerelle, both a key bridge and piece of art CHUM – Largest Healthcare Project in North America. (2018) Credit: CannonDesign + NEUF Architect(e)s.

also producing or making more, in a digital sense. Anthony might tell a team member:

> Hey, I know you used to do this with SketchUp. But try it now with *this* because now we can easily bring it into our BIM platform. Let's try this out because now when you sketch we can pass it on more quickly to our client and get feedback.

Anthony explains:

> There are always different methods that will require a computational specialist to stand between, and understand how, we can disseminate knowledge. Part of that requires our being on top of the latest technology and processes, and actually using them. This ferrets out three options: we can buy the tool, once somebody makes it; we can hire somebody else who can do this better, which architects do all the time for a lot of different reasons; or we can do it – create the tool – ourselves. My thinking is: I'm really glad to buy that tool. My job, most of the time, is to tell somebody to buy that tool.

Challenges of leading design technologists

The architect's problem is a leadership problem: one that has to do with leading individuals and teams into the emerging future. The questions are still there. Do technology leaders need to learn and use the technology? What do technology leaders need to understand, and why? What are some of the special challenges of leading design technologists? Are design technologists more/less easily bored than other employees? Are design technologists more/less utilized than other employees? "Distractions will consume your time that could be better spent on other things," says Ryan Cameron, Project Architect at DLR Group. He continues:

When you do find something, pursue it with everything you have. You have 1,140 minutes in a day; use them wisely. Anyone can be under-utilized or bored by what they do if they do it too long. They are utilized when leadership fully embraces and understands the capacity that Superusers bring to the business.

If we had a phenomenal hand drafter from 1982 and a phenomenal person in 2012 using a BIM authoring tool and asked them to produce the same building, who would produce more work? Who would grow bored? Who would be faster or better? I don't know what the ratio would be, but I do know it wouldn't be 1:1. It might be something like 1:16. So that person might get done in a day what the other might take two weeks to accomplish. What does that person do with their time? Now we ask, take that same 2012 person and pit them against someone from 2042. It's not even close. So instead of being bored, take that extra time you have and use it to get closer to that future design technologist.

What keeps design technology leaders up at night?

Design technology leaders may not concern themselves with the day-to-day tasks of specialists, but that doesn't mean they don't have concerns of their own. What keeps firm leaders up at night? Among their frequent concerns are messaging and finding the right words to communicate, solving the right problems, the next thing, and even the fear of success.

Messaging

It might come as a surprise to design technologists that their leaders sweat over *wordsmithing* – how things are communicated – to their troops and fellow leadership. "The biggest one that's kept me up at night has been, how do I phrase these changes?" says Shane Burger, Principal and Global Leader of Technical Innovation at Woods Bagot. He continues:

How do I talk about these changes in the industry, whether it's a process change, or a product change with digital culture? How do I talk about that with our lead designers, who don't necessarily work with all of the latest digital tools? How do I keep them engaged in the conversation? That's the thing that keeps me up the most.

Sure, there are emails and other important things that come through. But for me, it's very specific ways things get phrased. On more than one occasion, I've woken up in the middle of the night with a turn of a phrase. I've gotten up to write it down. Speaking to designers, who often work conceptually, I need to speak conceptually. But I also need to tie it down to their projects. It does keep me up at night thinking specifically about how to do those things. And even more so, what are the things I need to start advocating for change in our business model in the practice to make sure we stay relevant?

Design technology leaders have to choose their words carefully, in part because they're privy to things in the pipeline, or coming up in the near future. Software manufacturers have hyped technology to the point where one becomes immune to the hype, in terms of thinking about the effect it can have for one's organization. Language and choosing one's words wisely plays a significant role when leading teams. "What has worked for me is just being very honest, transparent and the exercise of common sense," says Hilda Espinal. She continues:

One must choose one's words carefully, especially to not over-promise and under-deliver, not offend anyone, and all of that I do in the day-to-day conversations. But, in terms of being honest and being able to manage expectations, that's where someone like myself becomes key in the role that I'm in. Because some vendors and other people misrepresent themselves. It's super important to carry conversations intelligently and informedly, talk about the potential realistically, challenge them if something seems suspect.

It's important to point out that messaging works both ways. Specialists also need to be careful not to overhype technology to their leaders. "I am very blessed to have very open and supportive leadership, but I am careful to not over-sell my proposals," says HCM's Jordan Billingsley. "This comes from a sensitivity of BIM being oversold as THE solution without properly addressing the necessary business changes that accompanied the technology shift from CAD to BIM."

Solving the right problems

Firm leaders often ask *what is advancing in our space that we are not seeing*? Dan Anthony says:

> What keeps me up – the fear – is, what am I not seeing? I want the things we do to be effective. The techniques we develop to be effective. My worry is, are we solving trivial problems? Or are we part of something that's going to make the design space better? Ultimately, a lot of us are interested in improving the way the whole process happens. The process of building things in the world, and the way we do them specifically in our culture or in AEC, are a mess. And could be a lot better, and better for the planet. And be a lot more responsive to actual outcomes. My worry is that we're not actually getting there. We're getting further down a path. That keeps me up.
>
> I'm concerned that we might be rolling out more bad buildings and not buildings that are going to help solve the climate crisis. One of our important activities is analytics. Being clear-minded, and not lying to ourselves about outcomes. We'll go through the process of making something and at the end of the day ask, does this have a positive influence? We have to spend the time to do analytics and ask, did this really have the effect we expected it to have? Yes? No? Should we do more of this? Should we do less of this? Sometimes, you'll work on something for a long time and find out it's not actually solving the problem that you started out to solve. The only way you are going to understand what to do next time, or what to do better, is to do a post-mortem of the project. In the end, hopefully creating a better skillset or organizational structure. So that the next time you take on a project, you inform your decisions based on something that didn't work last time.
>
> One thing I hope for is that so much lives within that kind of singularity of project findings. We often only look at our own past experiences. I would love to find a way to learn more from what other people and firms do as well. One of the things that is going to move our industry further is if we look at a way to understand the outcomes of not just our work, but of other people's work as well. There's going to be a better way to share that knowledge in the future – I just don't know what it is.

The next thing

"I'm almost always thinking about the next thing," says Hilda Espinal. "I am relatively new to the firm. It's just, how am I going to design this? What is my next move, what is my next thing to stay ahead of the competition? Always thinking about that." She continues:

> What's that next thing that others maybe thought of but haven't pursued, or maybe have not even thought about? How do I lead? There is also the less strategic but time-consuming day-to-day stuff, like what's due tomorrow also next week, type thing. I have staff I work with closely. They are very talented and sometimes I think about what can I do to retain them while continuing to develop them and hence, [be] more attractive to others. What can we do to better the work that we do, the stuff that we went to school for, for our careers in architecture, so there's not an exodus?

For other firm leaders, the concern centers around, how will a new initiative scale? Cory Brugger, CTO of HKS says:

> For us, if we put a new initiative in place, say we're going to do x, y, and z for our design process. Here's our pilot, we define the complete workflow, we run the project through the paces, we verify results, and document the process. How do we implement across 24 offices? Who is responsible for it? So, there have been plenty of initiatives started, but for an initiative to be a success or have a firm-wide impact, on a market or on the effectiveness of our delivery process, we need to create resonance and get buy-in from our staff. How can we disseminate and ensure that an initiative takes hold without personal investment? I'm not there yet.
>
> That's one of the most important things for us to address. If you want to have process change, organizational change, or application of new tools and processes, you need champions on every project. You cannot rely on having a single person in an office to help nudge, or you'll end up doing trophy one-off projects. That's good for those projects, but I'm focused on how you implement change across an organization.

Fear of success

Some design technology leaders are so fearless in their approach to practice, one can't imagine anything that keeps them up at night. Still, in a position of leadership, one can feel an inordinate amount of responsibility for those they work with, within their organizations, and even beyond. "I'm not afraid to fail," admits Ryan Cameron, in reference to a new automation tool he was working on at the time. "I'm afraid to succeed. So the truth would be, what if the thing that I'm making ends up collapsing the whole professional process? That's my concern. That's all on me."

Design technology leader provenance

Leader provenance, like art provenance, traces leadership roles back to their origin point, usually in IT or design. The air is thin for design technology leaders – there are so few people in these roles, and for those who have made it to the top, they more often than not arrive there by way of IT (CTO, CIO) or traditional roles (project designer, project architect, project manager) and not via design technology itself. "It's crucial to have people at the director level that can drive and speak to the need of having a computational designer in the industry, because they're solving problems," says Thornton Tomasetti's Hiram Rodriguez. "They are solving hardcore problems in the industry and it is crucial to have them."

As Dan Anthony said earlier:

My role is both defined and amorphous. The official title on paper is that I am a Design Computation Leader at the firm level. Which puts me under our Chief Information Officer, Paul Audsley, who leads NBBJ's technology strategy and operations in the

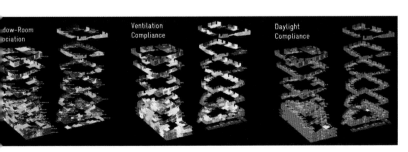

Figure 9.3
The Eleventh: live spatial analysis. (2018) Credit: Woods Bagot.

179

areas of design, building information modeling, design computation, infrastructure, security and project collaboration. Myself and two other people, currently Marc Syp and Nate Holland, are Design Computation Leaders. We sit in different studios. Our goal is to organize all of the different efforts in every studio across the firm. There are currently about 12 people in our group that do this kind of work, with the three of us leading the way.

Anthony sees being a Design Computation Leader similar to being an enlightened BIM manager. "Yes, right now we treat computational method as a compliment to BIM," continues Anthony:

In some ways, it's an artificial distinction, and becoming more and more so every day. But at the same time, we have a BIM manager on a project. They end up being a little more tactical due to their role. BIM managers are often also more useful day-to-day, since computation isn't always in play in a project.

It helps if your boss is a former design technologist. Having been in your shoes, they're more likely to equip design technologists for success. Call this *design technology leadership advocacy*. Anthony continues:

I work closely with NBBJ Design partner and co-lead of the firm's corporate practice, Ryan Mullenix, the partner in my studio. Part of the reason my role exists is because of Ryan's advocacy. His interest in computation being part of our practice. I owe a lot to both Ryan and those who came before me in this role in that it creates a space for this in our design practice. While Ryan is our design director and leader across all of the projects that happen in our studio, he's not necessarily involved in the day-to-day of all of them. In his role he looks for opportunities to apply our computational process and kind of thinking to more workplace projects.

Mullenix's background in computation makes him sensitive to, and have an appreciation for, the needs for the technology in NBBJ's practice. Anthony says:

The key about Ryan is that he understands that there is a value to letting the exploration take place. We have other studios in our company that now have design computation leaders that don't come from a similar computation background. The difference between the studios is that Ryan will look for the value in it and apply the value in the process. In other firms where that isn't the case, it's harder to change the fundamental construction of how they execute their design process to allow room for any kind of visual or performance exploration of analysis. Let's trust our intuition but inform our intuition with more information if we can. It impacts how things are communicated, in a wider stance, the things we already know about design. Expressing and proving to our clients that there's a value to not just doing things the cheap way but doing things in a way that is going to maximize the views, or fresh air, or the proximity. A lot of our clients think in a way that is not artistic. They're essentially saying: demonstrate that this will make things better in our building or we're not going to do it. And so we demonstrate it.

Figure 9.4
The Eleventh: panels automatically generated in Revit. (2018) Credit: Woods Bagot.

181

Staying ahead of the learning curve

Each firm leader has a different process for how they keep up with technology. Some design technology leaders proactively seek out new technologies to understand – some reactively, by waiting for others to bring them to their attention. "There is definitely a proactive element," says Anthony. He continues:

> One thing that I personally feel deficient in is that I don't always stay socially active, for example, on Twitter. Part of it is that I sometimes have a hard time getting through the chaff of it – there is a lot of noise in that space. But I do think following asocial media is important – I do track it. Research is another very important part of this. And I do a lot of research. It's about leaving space to explore what's available. It's part of my job to do this. It's not time that I have on the books. But something I think is critical to succeed at my job. A lot of times we have these clear goals where we really want to figure out a way for doing something. The risk for us is that we start down a path where we're trying to reinvent the wheel. I grew up with the Internet as a way of solving that problem by searching for that information. Reaching out to people, asking them questions, is a great way to solve that problem. The key is that you do a really thorough job of exploring what the state of affairs is, by digging through GitHub, by reading journals to see if anyone has tried to solve this before.

The third space: leading not just the firm but the transformation

Some – the first users – will want to lead the technology transformation, while others – the survivors – will be happy coping with it. The rest – call them victims – will be the casualties of it when it's forced on them. "I want to be a first user," says Anthony:

> I want to use it when it doesn't work. When you imagine what it could be. And you have to scrape and scrap to find the right button that does the thing that you actually want it to do. Just the other day I was loading up the new Dynamo in Formit, and finding that it wasn't working. There was some server bug in

there. I was thinking, well, someday this is going to be exactly what I want it to be. I like that feeling. But that is definitely true about the three types of people. What we're going to see fairly soon, is people who want to keep designing the way design happens now. When you think about us and the vendors, there's this third space that's there. Which is where design is actually the design of the process and the tools. There's this whole space in the middle where more and more the techniques you use are becoming the outcome of the design. It is a third space and it is for everybody to capture. I am really interested in filling in that space.

One of the risks people keep talking about is that designers are going to lose agency, that design is going to go to processes that you can implement, that do some of the design for you. The development of that kind of technology is fascinating because it doesn't fit into our neat model where these people make the software and we're the people who design things and who use that software. There's a space where there's a chance to be a designer, decide what you want to automate, decide what you want to control, and what your goal is. The real truth is that the goal of architecture will continue to be to make things work the best for the lowest price.

We manage these transformations and what the outcome looks like because new techniques will make buildings look different and function different than they do now. While still upholding the goals of what you design for. There is some kind of person in the middle that is a designer and knows what the intentions are of making human space that isn't purely one or the other of the two things.

Marketing technology capabilities

Having mentioned TT CORE, HKS LINE and LMNts, tech-forward firms have, since the late 2000s, for a number of reasons, introduced tech labs. One has been to promote the firm as innovative. Brian Ringley says:

From what I've seen, those groups are legitimate efforts to help improve the way teams work. I don't think I've ever seen a team at

a firm and thought, "That's completely fake." I don't actually think that leadership would tolerate that at architecture firms. They would see that fluff and they'd want to slice it off, but I do think that they take some of the more superficial things that those teams do and trumpet those. Woods Bagot Design Technology did this, too. We released a tool and that was nice marketing for us. It's a contribution to the culture that we've taken so much from, but if "what Brian and Andrew did with Wombat was their primary contribution to architecture while they were at Woods Bagot," I would be bothered. I feel like it was the workflows, the frameworks with which we engaged the project teams to solve complex problems.

Some firms need to bring in someone into the sales meeting who knows technology and they'll do their five-minute tech commercial. But the minute you get the job you never hear from them again. "Right, or, just in case someone asks questions they are not comfortable answering," says Hilda Espinal. She continues:

But no, that is not the kind of pursuits I've been a part of. Recently at CannonDesign, my and my Digital Practice Director's engagement and contribution have been pivotal. But, it's so interesting because it's the mixture that I have with architecture and technology that is of interest. It's not the same if we're just going to talk about integrating networks and security and all that stuff which I've done in "previous lives." I can speak to that regard as well, it hardly ever comes up. The flavor of technology that is front and center of these recent conversations is what I call Technology in Practice, in capitals as that is what I am naming my CannonDesign Technology Innovation Group.

At times, design technologist specialists are brought into a client meeting unannounced, and often unprepared. They're told they're going to perform – say, as a computational designer – for them or they're going to run something that someone in the room can't do. "It depends on whom we're meeting with and show the different things that we have done in the past," says Hiram Rodriguez. He continues:

We have a good work sample folder with where we store images, videos, and presentations of various projects. So if it's a developer, we'll probably show VR and some automation processes of generating different schemes so we can calculate body carbon or rationalize column placement. Maybe an architect is more interested in rationalizing façades. We have workflows that show that. Moreover, the way you show it is different, because you want to be visual with the architect in terms of the variation you're going to have on the form, whereas with the developer you want to show metrics, tonnages, and pricing and all those components, whereas with the contractor and on site you want to show something about drones and site surveying.

Leading by empowering

How can firm leaders make the work exciting so that people want to come in to work, not only for their firm but in the industry? One way is by empowering employees. Leading design technologists requires a spirit of empowerment, engagement, and entrepreneurship. "A concept I am borrowing from successful contractors, speaking at a conference is that of rotation," explains Hilda Espinal, where employees rotate within the organization. "It would be amazing to grow as the-full-encompassing-whole-architect, by getting to some of this and some of that. Keeping it varied and hence, more interesting." Espinal continues:

You get to shadow or have exposure to different areas of the office and process. Maybe you get to work on something new for a little bit. And maybe you'll like it, maybe you'll hate it. Some people hate writing Specifications, some enjoy it. Maybe you work on the schematic portion of a project, because a lot of times you're getting pigeonholed as being a technical architect, so flex that conceptual muscle. But as architects it can also materialize by rotating between different market sectors or project delivery phases.

"Luckily at my firm there's this spirit of entrepreneurship, which is probably why I fit in so well," says Jordan Billingsley. He continues:

Whether you are a principal or a senior associate, you have probably retained a client or two, and the firm does not try to take that client away from you, they don't get involved with anything that you're doing, they just say, "Okay, here you go, we're basically just your legal support, and you just focus on customer service." Entrepreneurship has descended down to other aspects of the office, so they've been more open to people who present goals that they want to pursue personally. I feel very well supported at my firm, and I do know that that's a unique case, and they don't see it as risk whereas other people at other firms might see it as a risk.

What Billingsley does in this office today benefits from his having been an entrepreneur with Blackline. "I know how to make proposals, I know what it's like to present yourself in a way that is convincing to other people," says Billingsley. "And I'm self-motivated. Not that other people aren't, but I don't need direction to get something started." As with other Superusers, one can't necessarily just plug into a role and rise in an organization. Like an entrepreneur, it's still a blue ocean they're creating, one that remains a *risk journey*.

Epilogue

Automation and its discontents

UNStudio's Ben van Berkel predicts, "in the future all architecture practices will become arch tech firms, but for now we have to pave the way to make this expansion of our knowledge and expertise possible."[1] We as a profession and industry are about to come face to face with the onslaught of technological disruption, and remaining agile – irrespective of firm size or focus, maintaining an ability to pivot on a dime – in the face of change will be all the more important in the years ahead. Hiring and retaining good people who are flexible – who possess the requisite skillsets and mindsets – will remain imperative. Your having read to this point, just what these are ought to be clear and more certain.

In addition to everything else we do, firms today must also be software practices and technology firms – even if it's not in their DNA – creating apps and other digital tools, for their own use and commercialized for others. One reason beyond increased productivity is employee retention. AEC is undergoing a brain drain, where design firms compete for the best people not only with other design firms but also with software developers and startups. In lieu of traditional practice, recent graduates are going into arguably more alluring, lucrative startups, quicker-paced software development companies and verticals. How do we keep talented, smart people interested in a field where projects can take three to six years or more to complete? Understanding what makes Supersusers tick is an important first step. With the very entrepreneurial so-called Gen-Z generation poised to enter the workforce in the coming years, the internal development of new technologies and the potential commercialization of these tools will become more important in terms of retaining this talent.

Emerging design professionals – if we play our cards right, tomorrow's future Superusers – are concerned about their prospects for a bright and prosperous future. The concern isn't that "the robots will take over." Warranted or not, the concern for emerging professionals is that they want to develop entry-level, foundational skills. They're afraid that, by AI doing this "drudgery work" for them, the deskilling of practice that frees them "to work on design and be creative" instead keeps them from developing into well-rounded professionals who in their work experience flow. We owe it to ourselves, and to our clients, to be cognizant – but not anxious, panicked, or alarmed. As firm leaders, we need to talk about AI not in terms of survival, but instead, how we're going to leverage, exploit, embrace, and capitalize on the changes. It's not enough to "adapt" and "survive." As firm leaders, we must persevere – and have a vision, a plan, for how this will come about.

There is a strongly held belief by firm leaders that design technologists, when required, can always learn the tools, but becoming adept at people skills, on the other hand, requires constant nurturing and attention. Any investment in time, energy, and resources to improve communication skills – including interpersonal, conversational, and question-asking skills – as well as thought leadership,

Figure 10.1 Stephen Van Dyck and Scott Crawford, along with Jack Chaffin, founded Frankenstein Inc. in 2012 in order to purchase and operate a kit-built CNC mill they built in Scott's garage. Their work with that machine produced many studies and mockups for their concurrent work at LMN Architects and was the proof-of-concept that forged the way for LMN's full-blown shop which has become a key contributor to the firm's design process. (2018) Credit: Scott Crawford.

storytelling ability, and teachability, will prove worthwhile. As this book has tried to make clear, what separates Superusers from someone who specializes in technology is their interpersonal intelligence – their now famous finesse when it comes to human interaction. It's their consideration for other's interests, needs, and constraints that truly separate Superusers from ordinary technologists.

Figure 10.2 **Using their CNC machine, LMN Architects built several mockups of Voxman's Theatroacoustic System to validate their design and fabrication data for use in final construction. (2018) Credit: LMN Architects.**

Superusers' roles, as either generalists or specialists, fall into predictable categories, but are of exponentially more value when they fall along a continuum. Teams and firms benefit from the grey space of the Superuser's generalist/specialist hybrid role. They deliver value by means of increased productivity, via agile processes, and automating repetitive processes. Superusers provide an improved user experience, by easing tool use and accessibility, while connecting tools, people, and processes, reducing user pain points.

But Superusers can't help firms if they can't be found. The search for design technologists needs to be ongoing, requiring never-ending vigilance, and begins the moment after one is hired – not when the need arises, or worse, well past. Don't discount growing from within. Turning current employees into tool-virtuous, soft-skilled Superusers requires the same vigilance, determination, and creativity – it is every bit a design challenge as designing buildings – in coming up with an amicable plan for all involved. Firm leaders must decide how much of the risk in the Superuser's risk journey they are willing to share.

Team leaders were once thought clueless by their direct reports when giving a team member a month-long assignment, and because they didn't understand what's involved, telling them *it'll only take a day*. Today, with computation, team leaders are equally clueless when giving a team member a daylong assignment, and because they don't understand automation, tell them *it'll take a month*. Understanding what Superusers actually *do* all day to earn their coveted appellation ought to be on the top of managers' and team leaders' priorities.

Turning a two- to three-day assignment into a 20-minute step is why we automate in the first place. It also frees you – and your direct reports – to focus on designers' core competency. Firms need to continue to automate what they repetitively generate manually, then look through their standard delivery processes to see how much more they can automate. Today we can automate the manual calculation parts of design, addressing ergonomic standards, legal code requirements for life safety, and so much more – so, automate. But as Ian Keough, the founder of Dynamo and author of this book's Foreword suggests: *Architecture isn't what's left over after everything's been automated*.

Keeping Superusers, and keeping them from leaving for richer pastures – especially when design firms cannot be expected to match

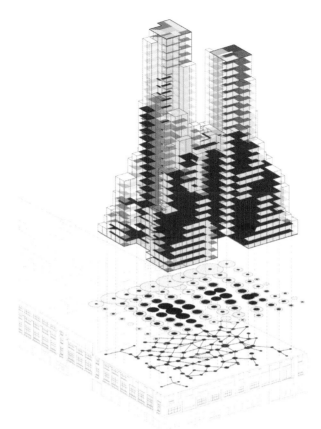

Figure 10.3
3D optimization support calculation for a new building. (2018) Credit: Thornton Tomasetti Core Studio.

startup salaries – is an ongoing concern. Think in terms of intrinsic rewards. While intrinsic rewards won't pay back student loans, consider their role in career longevity, which if personal experience is any indication, can over time match startup salaries. Having a job that offers the opportunity to leverage your core competency every day on the job has a dollar equivalent. Think not just in terms of pay scale but the total package: all of the benefits of working as a design professional, including access to learning, personal and professional growth – not on apps and spreadsheets but on the hands-on model making that led to that mixed-use project going up down the street from your kid's school. As I tell my students, *always have a minor to go along with your major*. Only for design professionals, your *major* is what you do M-F. At the annual review, ask your employees, *what did you minor in this year*? Your minor is what will keep you relevant – and frankly fun to work with.

It is high time firms invest in, engage, and clear a path for Superusers, for what they are: the next generation of the profession.

Who better to take us into this future than the Superusers we work with?

Note

1 Marcus Fairs, UNStudio launches tech startup to drag architecture into "the age of the iPhone," *Dezeen*, March 12, 2018.

Index